D1121908

10% LESS DEMOCRACY

10%

LESS

DEMOCRACY

WHY YOU SHOULD

TRUST ELITES

A LITTLE MORE

AND THE MASSES

A LITTLE LESS

GARETT JONES

STANFORD UNIVERSITY PRESS • STANFORD, CALIFORNIA

STANFORD UNIVERSITY PRESS
Stanford, California

Printed in the United States of America on acid-free, archival-quality paper

Library of Congress Cataloging-in-Publication Data

Names: Jones, Garett, author.
Title: 10% less democracy: why you should trust elites a little more and the masses a little less / Garett Jones.
Other titles: 10 percent less democracy | Ten percent less democracy
Description: Stanford, California : Stanford University Press, 2020. | Includes bibliographical references and index.
Identifiers: LCCN 2019013942 (print) | LCCN 2019017660 (ebook) | ISBN 9781503603578 | ISBN 9781503603578 (cloth; alk. paper) | ISBN 9781503611214 (ebook)
Subjects: LCSH: Democracy. | Representative government and representation. | Elite (Social sciences) | Economic policy.
Classification: LCC JC423 (ebook) | LCC JC423 .J695 2020 (print) | DDC 321.8—dc23
LC record available at https://lccn.loc.gov/2019013942

Cover design: Rob Ehle

Text design: Kevin Barrett Kane

Typeset at Stanford University Press in 10/15 ITC Galliard Pro

*À prendre le terme dans la rigueur
de l'acception, il n'a jamais existé
de véritable démocratie, & il n'en
existera jamais.*

In the strict sense of the term, a
genuine Democracy never has
existed, and never will exist.

JEAN-JACQUES ROUSSEAU

Contents

10% LESS DEMOCRACY

INTRODUCTION

The Source of My Idea

ONCE I GOT THE CALL FROM CAMPUS POLICE, I knew I needed to write this book.

It was spring semester 2015, and I'd recently given a brief talk to a student group at my university. Natalie Schulhof, a reporter for the student newspaper, *Fourth Estate*, had come to the event and reported on my talk, entitled "10% Less Democracy." That was the first time I'd spoken at any length about this book's central idea: that in most of the rich countries, we've taken democracy, mass voter involvement in government, at least a little too far. We'd likely be better off if we kept the voters and even the elected officials a little further away from the levers of power. Let the government insiders run more of the show. After all, the insiders don't have to be perfect for 10% less democracy to be an improvement; they just have to be better than the voters.[1]

About a week after my talk, Schulhof's piece came out, quite thorough and extremely accurate, complete with a photo of me standing before the small student audience. From the article: "Garett Jones, associate economics professor at George Mason University, says that there should be less democracy in the United States. . . . Less democracy would lead to better governance."

But in our new age of social media, that article, accurate down to the last detail, wasn't the article that became widely shared online. Instead, the subsequent firestorm was fed by ideology-driven websites, with authors posting articles loosely based on *Fourth Estate*'s original piece but filling in the blanks of the short, accurate article with their own vitriol and blue-sky speculation. My personal favorite— precisely because it was so over the top—was penned by journalist and musician Ben Norton, who after decrying my lightly sketched proposals, concluded that "Jones is in many ways metonymic of the entire capitalist system he so faithfully admires. What makes Jones different from his economic ecclesiastical brethren is simply the fact that he has the chutzpah to openly say what so many other bourgeois economists are thinking deep-down."[2]

I'm quite happy to be told that I have chutzpah, and I'm also glad to be a metonymy—a symbolic stand-in—for much of anything! Alas, it appears my proposals weren't sufficiently offensive for Norton, since he had to invent a few of his own, and to then "wonder . . . if the neoliberal economist secretly thinks" a variety of revolting ideas that I vehemently oppose and won't deign to reprint here.

In the days after these ideology-driven websites wrote about my talk, I discovered a torrent of hate polluting both my email inbox and my Twitter account. I welcome disagreement with my ideas, and passionate disagreement is part of a healthy public debate, but for a brief period, I had my sole experience (so far!) as an object of profanity-laced Internet rage. It culminated in the call from campus police—and in my dozen years at George Mason, that was the first and still the only time I've received such a call. An officer left a voice-mail message, and I called back at my first opportunity. She said someone had left an angry voice mail criticizing me on a general campus phone number, and the officer noted with great discretion that the voice mail contained at least one profane expression. Was there anyone who might be upset with me lately? the officer asked.

I had an idea. And that idea became this book. So to the unknown person who left that voice mail, I offer my heartfelt gratitude. I dedicate this book to you.

A View from the Senate

Starting in summer 2002, I had the opportunity to spend a year as an economic policy adviser and legislative assistant to Senator Orrin Hatch of Utah. I've never had a better boss. You hear stories on Capitol Hill about senators who torment their staff, yelling, throwing tantrums, spreading their low-grade anger around the entire office, but Senator Hatch was overwhelmingly cheerful, even-keeled, and kind to those around him. He has elements of folksy charm, but far more than that, he has a now-rare quality of gentility. He especially loved the late senator Ted Kennedy. Whenever the two met—and they frequently did, sometimes just outside my office—they usually shared a big bear hug, no mere political shoulder-to-shoulder touch but the real thing.[3]

I learned a lot about real-world politics that year, even though I was by Capitol Hill standards not at all a powerful or influential staffer. I watched and learned, and in particular I listened. I've had two other shorter stints on the Hill. In 2004 I spent part of a summer working for the Senate side of the Joint Economic Committee, and earlier, in 1995, I spent six months as an intern to Senator Hatch during the first months of the Gingrich revolution. I've seen a lot on the Hill—enough stories to last a lifetime.

But here's the most important thing I learned: senators change their behavior dramatically when an election draws near. U.S. senators have six-year terms, and senators are broken into three classes, with one-third of them up for reelection every two years. Staff on the Senate side of Capitol Hill keep an eye on which senators are "in cycle"—less than two years out from an election. I recall a passing comment of a Senate staffer about a now-retired senator, relatively powerful, from the Midwest. I paraphrase my sixteen-year-old memory: "Oh, he's been voting to please the party the last four years, but now that he's in cycle he'll be heading right back toward the center."

Yes, it's obvious that senators behave differently when an election is around the corner, but if voters were easily duped, mere puppets manipulated by TV ads and a few handshakes, then a looming election would change the senator only superficially. More flights to the home state, more interviews with local TV, more ads with a waving flag and the senator's smiling family: those would be the sole signs that an election was coming. Superficial changes, not changes in substance.

But in the Senate we saw more than that, we saw senators voting differently, drafting different types of bills, wondering and worrying more about how actions in DC would go over back home. Senators act as if voters care about the recent past, with the emphasis on *recent*.

The lessons I drew from learning the value of long terms?

1. If you're hoping for politicians to be brave, don't hope for much in an election year.

2. If you'd like your politicians to be braver, have fewer election years.

The Euphemism

I was trained in monetary economics, and my early research was all about the different ways that the Federal Reserve, America's central bank, influences the U.S. economy. Much of this research focuses on how shifts in monetary policy—looser or tighter money, selling or buying U.S. government bonds—influence interest rates, business hiring, and total economic activity. Monetary economics is often the study of how certain government actions today shape the private sector in the future. But monetary economists have gone further and asked which kinds of government rules and which kinds of government bureaucracies are likely to cause better government actions. It's not just, "What's the right choice?" but also, "Who makes the better choices?"

Economists care so much about good outcomes that we often search further up the chain of causation. It's the same approach that medical doctors take when looking for ways to make people healthier. They start by looking for ways to cure disease, then for ways to prevent disease, and may end their quest by searching for the best public health programs to encourage vaccinations or to create safer tap water. The search for deep causes, root causes, may take us in unexpected directions.

Governments across rich countries have had widely differing rules about how to run monetary policy: gold standards, pegged exchange rates, vague promises of "price stability," and many others. And they have different kinds of bureaucracies implementing those policies. Some are about as detached from democracy as an appointed judge, while others work directly for the nation's prime minister and can be fired at any moment. Once monetary economists started looking into what kinds of government rules and government bureaucracies predicted economic success and which predicted economic tragedy, they found a repeated pattern: the more "independent" the nation's central bank was from the political process, the better things typically turned out. Note the quotation marks: the area of research is known as the "central bank independence" literature, but that's a euphemism. Good central banks tend to be independent, but independent from what? Mostly from voters.

The lessons I drew from learning about the value of central bank independence?

1. If you want good government policies, you'll often want them determined and enforced by anonymous bureaucrats, far from the reach of the voters.

2. If you want policy determined and enforced by anonymous bureaucrats—like judges, central bankers, or trade commissioners—don't say you want oligarchic, undemocratic bureaucrats in charge. Just say you want "independent" bureaucrats. It goes over much better.

Enhancing the Hive Mind

I spent about a decade researching the many ways in which smarter neighbors can improve our lives. My first book, *Hive Mind: How Your Nation's IQ Matters So Much More Than Your Own*, brings together that line of research. Through the process, I learned about the workings of the human brain, the value of intelligence tests, the merits and joys of listening to psychologists. *10% Less Democracy* has nothing to do with any of that, at least not directly. But one relevant lesson I did learn from that experience was that voter skill matters for the wealth of nations—that the clichés are true and that informed voters are an extremely important ingredient in the recipe for good government. Indeed, informed voters are so important that many thinkers—including economist Dambisa Moyo of Barclays and other corporate boards and philosopher Jason Brennan of Georgetown—have been searching for ways to give the most-informed voters greater weight in modern democracies. The push for "one person, one vote," come what may, has had both benefits and costs, and in the twenty-first century we have enough data to make it clear that the costs are pretty high. The costs of giving equal weight to the informed and uninformed alike are high enough that it's worthwhile to look for creative ways to tilt the scales just a little bit toward the informed.

This may be this book's most controversial claim, and if you conclude that the benefits of giving informed voters a little more weight are vastly outweighed by the costs, then I wholeheartedly encourage you to reject the proposals I offer. But I hope you'll take the time to first look at the evidence. You may decide that even if giving more weight to informed voters is a bad idea for your country, it might be a reasonable choice for the country next door.

The lessons I drew from thinking about the value of informed voters?

1. Rich democracies already de facto give more weight to the informed. Indeed, it's well known that the educated vote at higher rates. The core question is whether it would be wise to dial up this extra influence just a little.

2. If we want people to think carefully about the topic of voting reform, it's usually best to suggest that they try thinking about the question in the abstract—or about whether that reform might be a good idea in some other country. A little detachment goes a long way to spur objectivity.

Making the Case for 10% Better Governance

Economists have a reputation for assuming away the hard problems of social science—assuming that people are perfectly rational or that the government data we have in front of us are accurate enough to be useful. We tease each other about this. There's an old joke that economists tell to make the point:

> Three professors—a physicist, a chemist, and an economist—get stuck on a desert island, and just as things are looking desperate, a crate of canned goods washes up on the beach. Pinto beans, spinach, chicken, potatoes—all that and so much more. But they don't have an easy way to open the cans. So the three professors all offer their plans for opening the cans.
>
> First, the physicist:
>
> "If we climb the palm tree and drop the cans from a sufficient height to land on this particular rock, the cans will burst open, and we'll be able to eat."
>
> Second, the chemist:
>
> "Obviously, exploding cans aren't the way to go. Instead, I believe we can make an acidic paste from a mixture of dried palm leaves, ground-up shells, and sea salt. Pour the mixture over the lids, set in the sun, and over the course of a few days, the mixture will burn through the cans and we'll be able to eat.
>
> Finally, the economist:
>
> "Assume the existence of a can opener."

When life gives you lemons, economists have a reputation for assuming the existence of enough sugar and water to make lemonade. Sometimes that's a fair critique of my field. However, I think it's also a fair critique of other fields of inquiry as well, and the reason we economists get called on our absurd assumptions more often is mostly because we make our absurd assumptions easier to see. In economics, the math we use has a pleasant side effect: frequently—and I'd say usually—it makes it more difficult to hide bad reasoning. If you're trying to obfuscate, let me suggest that when talking to intelligent, well-informed audiences, verbal jargon works much better than equations.

But I don't want to obfuscate, and I don't want to assume my answer; that means that when I'm suggesting political reforms, they should be reforms that work in the real world, and I shouldn't be "assuming the can opener" of replacing democracy with enlightened dispassionate technicians. So I won't assume the can opener of meritocracy, of replacing control by voters with control by the perfectly wise. Instead, I assume that political reforms of the future will work a lot like political reforms of the past, warts and all. In the jargon of statistics I'll be staying "within the normal range of variation," staying in the real world.

Life is often about trade-offs, choosing one imperfect bundle of options rather than another. My job in the next ten chapters is to persuade you that if your nation enacts some of the political reforms I suggest, democracy-reducing reforms that take control of the state a little further away from the average citizen, your nation's bundle of joys and sorrows after the reforms will be better, all things considered, than the bundle of joys and sorrows your nation would've experienced otherwise. Whether I persuade you of the value of each reform, I think you'll be surprised by the joys you discover along the way—the joys of embracing, if only for a moment, if only in the privacy of your mind—the wisdom of slightly less democracy.

1 The Big Benefits of a Small Dose of Democracy

HERE'S ONE GREAT THING ABOUT DEMOCRACY: democracies don't let their citizens die in famines. Every country in the twentieth century that you can think of that experienced massive, rapid increases in death from hunger and starvation was something other than a functioning democracy. Maybe it was a dictatorship, or quite likely it was colonized by some other country—and in a few cases, it may have had a democratic government on paper, but it lacked a capable government, one up to the task of providing rapid services for its citizens. But for more than a century, widespread, rapid death from hunger has never happened in a country with a functioning government where the citizens had the right to choose their government's leaders.

It was the Nobel-winning economist Amartya Sen who made this bold claim, most famously and quite sweepingly in his excellent 1999 book, *Development as Freedom*: "No famine has ever taken place in the history of the world in a functioning democracy."[1] Other researchers have tried to beat up on Sen's finding, but they have failed. Of course, one wonders whether this is just a correlation, a repeated pattern that might be caused by some other factor like prosperity or low corruption. Here's one test, one that Sen himself used: compare what happens in a nation just before versus just after that nation becomes a democracy. India's last famine—the Bengal famine—occurred in

1943. India became an independent nation in 1947. After the end of British rule that year, India was still poor and its government was riddled with corruption. But Indians never again experienced widespread death from famine. Holding the country constant and changing the type of government from a colonial outpost to a new democracy was, it appears, all it took to save lives.

That's a strong argument for democracy, and it's one that I believe in. It has a twin argument, also based on over a century of real evidence: democracies don't engage in widespread slaughter of their own voting citizens. Government-led massacres are exceptionally rare within democracies. Economist William Easterly of New York University oversaw the creation of a new database on this topic with data from around the world, spanning 1820 to 1998. A key finding was that "in general, high democracy appears to be the single most important factor in avoiding large magnitudes of mass killings, as the highest quartile of the sample in democracy accounts for only 0.1% percent of all the killings."[2] Since this book is entitled *10% Less Democracy* and is targeted at nations that are already near the very highest levels of democracy, even embracing all of the reforms I suggest will keep these nations in the top quartile—the top 25 percent—and will keep them away from the risk of widespread mass killings.

Of course, as with the no-famines claim, there are caveats and provisos in the underlying research. In the case of famines, here's one recurring question: How many deaths from hunger in how short a time does it take to count as a famine? But the overall message is strong: democracies substantially reduce the risk of widespread, short-run death of a nation's citizens and overwhelmingly reduce the risk of government-backed massacres compared to other forms of real-world government.

So *some* level of democracy is a genuine lifesaver, but how much democracy do we need to get those lifesaving benefits? Not that much. Easterly showed that a country only needs to have a level of democracy in the global top 25% to eliminate 99.9% of deaths from government massacres. Sen himself concludes that to avoid famines, all you need is a government where the elections are genuinely competitive—the political parties are genuinely allowed to argue their case in public and the vote counting is reasonably fair—and where the press is reasonably free—one that is free enough, for example, to report whether people are going hungry somewhere in the country. Competitive elections and a free press: that's enough to prevent famines in Sen's view. And throughout the rest of this book, no reform I suggest will tamper with those minimum requirements. So while I'll suggest quite a few ways to reduce the power of voters in the course of this book—longer term lengths for politicians, giving government bondholders a formal role in running the country, or handing more power over to independent government agencies, for instance—none of those reforms will tamper with competitive elections or a free press.

Democracy as a Luxury Good

You might suspect that one strong argument for democracy is that democracies tend to be richer than nondemocracies. And as a raw correlation, a pattern in the data, that's certainly true. But as with Sen's famine-avoiding case for democracy, we need to check out other possible explanations for this pattern. Is it the democracy that causes the prosperity? Does giving citizens a voice in government encourage the government to enlarge the pie faster? Or perhaps it's that prosperity creates conditions that turn autocracies and monarchies into democracies. That last theory is known as the Lipset hypothesis, after the great sociologist Seymour Martin Lipset. He argued in 1959 that as nations get richer, they tend to have larger middle classes, and these middle classes more or less naturally tend to become politically organized and start to pressure the government to listen to their demands. As he summarized his view, "The more well-to-do a nation, the greater the chances that it will sustain democracy."[3] An economist might summarize Lipset's story by saying that perhaps democracy is a luxury good, and as the average person in a nation gets richer, she is more likely to buy this luxury good.

Let's take some time to look at how social scientists have tested theories of the relationship between democracy and economic performance. For instance, consider whether economies tend to grow faster or slower within a few years of becoming a democracy. Is there pro-democracy evidence as clear as Sen's on famines? No. Overall, countries that make a transition to democracy don't grow any faster (or slower) compared to beforehand. So that kind of clear test isn't helping the case that democracy is causing prosperity.

That isn't the only kind of test one can run. One can also compare countries that start off similar along a variety of measures—countries that are, for instance, just as far from the equator, and just as rich, and that start with similar education levels—and then check to see if *within that group*, the nations that are more democratic tend to grow faster over the next few decades. In effect, this is what the statistical method known as multivariate regression can do for us. There are endless statistical tests checking to see if democracies grow faster than otherwise similar nondemocracies, and this academic literature gives a clear answer: there is no clear answer. There is no professional consensus at all on whether higher levels of democracy cause higher growth, cause slower growth, or cause nothing much at all. Government professor John Gerring of the University of Texas at Austin and coauthors reviewed both the before-and-after evidence and the multivariate, cross-country evidence as it stood in 2005: "The *net* effect of democracy on growth performance cross-nationally over the last five decades is negative or null."[4]

That means that it's possible that democracy is actually bad for the economy—truly a luxury good—or it might be a wash, but Gerring's read of the evidence is that it's hard to argue that democracy is genuinely good for economic performance. Here, the big correlation between democracy and prosperity isn't a sign of causation. But do case studies—anecdote-driven reviews of historical patterns—tell a more optimistic story about democracy causing growth? No: "For the most part, case study approaches to this question confirm the results of cross-national growth empirics."[5]

One widely discussed paper coauthored by famed MIT economist Daron Acemoglu is provocatively entitled "Democracy Does Cause Growth," so you can guess the main finding.[6] Like many other papers, it draws on cross-country evidence and analyzes the evidence statistically rather than anecdotally, but its measure of democracy is exceptionally crude: It's a simple zero-one indicator. In the Acemoglu view, either you're a democracy or you're not, with no gray area in between. But what I'm contending over the next nine chapters is that it's the *degree* of democracy that matters. This is a book about the gray area.

Voting for Dog Catcher

The most famous ancient democracy, that of Athens, set a high bar for citizen involvement. Democracy there meant that every free male citizen of Athens could vote, in person, on every piece of legislation the government considered. Every major job in government was elective as well—that is, if it wasn't filled through random selection, like modern jury duty. So both personnel *and* policy were debated publicly and voted on publicly. The Athenians would surely never have considered our modern "democracies" to be anything of the sort. We vote for representatives who then go on to make key government decisions for years before having to check back in with the voters. The Athenian citizens, by contrast, voted not only to recall key military leaders right in the middle of their war with Sparta but also to fire them. That's how Thucydides, one of the dismissed Athenian generals, wound up with enough time on his hands to write his famed *History of the Peloponnesian War*. The modern equivalent of Athenian democracy would be voting on legislation with our smartphones: voting amendment by amendment on each piece of legislation, and voting on potential government appointments after watching Facebook Live hearings where the nominees get grilled by citizens submitting interview questions from across the nation. We could all vote on interest rate changes while we're at it. Thanks to technology, 100% democracy is nearly possible.

However, outside of the classic New England town meeting, nobody today expects democracy to mean citizens voting on every government decision. No international democracy index declares a nation "less democratic" just because the dog catcher is appointed by the mayor rather than elected by the citizens. Instead, it's widely taken for granted, in theory and practice, that "democracy" refers not just to direct democracy—with voter referenda on legislation and elections for every government job—but also to indirect democracy—with voters choosing between competing candidates or competing political parties, who in turn will go off and run the actual government for a few years before returning to check back in with the voters.

But once we recognize that fact—that "democracy" can refer to more than one type of widespread citizen involvement in governing—that opens the door to asking what kind of democracy works best for people. And note that nowhere here am I taking it for granted that democracies are *by definition* governments that respect individual rights, have a reasonably fair rule of law, provide universal mass education, or include any other particular set of norms or policy outcomes. I'm following the standard late twentieth-century definition of democracy, perhaps made most famous by Yale's Robert Dahl. In his words, democracy combines:

1. Effective participation [in the political process]
2. Equality in voting
3. Gaining enlightened understanding [This is hard; Dahl knows.]
4. Exercising final control over the agenda [Voting is no mere empty ceremony.]
5. Inclusion of [nearly all] adults[7]

So in scholarly usage, "democracy" does not refer to a set of ideal policies or an ideal set of institutions or cultural norms. It just means widespread, substantive voter involvement in governance—with enough cognitive equality across citizens so that people can make informed choices. Not "the right" choices by some moral standard, just informed choices.

A nation can in principle be democratic and have no welfare state, a high level of corruption, or a legal system that discriminates against minority groups. Indeed, this last concern—that democracy would lead to the "tyranny of the majority"—was at the forefront of traditional concerns about democracy. The American founding fathers were famously concerned about this possibility; James Madison's *Federalist No. 51* offers the classic formulation of the problem. This indeed is why over the centuries, many thinkers have pushed to place limits on full-blown democracy—perhaps in the form of a written constitution, a bill of rights, or an independent judiciary—limits that would, to use Duke historian Nancy MacLean's expression, place "Democracy in Chains." Over the course of this book, I'll consider just which types of chains on modern democracies—heavy or light, with locks that are easy or hard to pick—are likely to lead to better social outcomes.

Democracy, Trade, and Peace

Since democracy refers to widespread citizen involvement in the process of governing—not to good policy outcomes—then whether democracy raises the probability of achieving your ideal policies, my ideal policies, or someone else's ideal policies is an empirical question. We'll have to look at the evidence, and the best form of evidence will rarely be an anecdote or a case study. The best form of evidence in practice will be thoughtful cross-country or before-and-after comparisons—and I've already noted that on the overall question of democracy and economic performance, there's apparently no there there.

There's another important area where there's apparently no there there, or at least no robust, clear result: the link between democracy and peace. Again, as with democracy and overall economic performance, there's a clear, simple pattern in decades of data: democracies are definitely less likely to go to war with each other, and they may even be less likely to go to war overall. As political scientists Mark Bell of the University of Minnesota and Kai Quek of the University of Hong Kong put it in a 2018 article, "The 'democratic peace'—the regularity that democracies rarely (if ever) fight with other democracies but do fight with nondemocracies—is one of the most famous findings in international relations scholarship."[8]

Some interpret this correlation as a simple case of cause-and-effect: citizens don't like the thought of sending their children into battle, so they discourage politicians from starting wars. Furthermore, democracies have a variety of institutions, formal and informal, that they can use to engage with other democracies and defuse potential conflict; the norms of democracy may have the power to shape international relations. This theory that democracy itself lowers the probability of war—at least with other democracies, and maybe overall—is known as the "democratic peace hypothesis."

But again, one should wonder whether some other factor is doing the heavy lifting. And indeed, another good story fits the facts relatively well: the "liberal peace hypothesis." The story goes that nations with broadly liberal institutions—in the traditional European sense of liberal, with a mix of market institutions, citizens with a wide range of civil liberties, widespread trade with other nations, and a neutral, reasonably fair rule of law—tend to have fewer wars in part because wars disrupt valuable trade relationships. The economist Albert Hirschman reviewed related arguments from the seventeenth and eighteenth centuries in his outstanding book, *The Passions and the Interests: Political Arguments for Capitalism Before Its Triumph*.[9] He noted that Enlightenment-era thinkers believed that capitalism would tend to make men less aggressive and more willing to cooperate, since entrepreneurial thinking is more about win-win relationships than about win-lose relationships. These theories show up in economist John Maynard Keynes's quip that it's better for men to tyrannize over their bank accounts than over each other.

Some versions of this "liberal peace" hypothesis focus particularly on trade relationships. One set of results finds that both trade and democracy appear to predict lower rates of armed conflict:

"We find increasingly strong support for the liberals' belief that economic interdependence [between nations] and democracy have important pacific benefits."[10] This is noteworthy, since as we shall see in the next chapter, democracies aren't all that enthusiastic about freer trade, so there may be a cruel trade-off between having more democracy and more liberal trade policies, both of which may be paths to peace

In the fiftieth-anniversary issue of the Journal of Peace Research, Håvard Hegre of Uppsala University and Peace Research Institute Oslo noted, "Perhaps the most serious challenge to the democratic peace comes from arguments suggesting that both democracy and peace are outcomes of more fundamental societal changes. Most of these are associated with socioeconomic development." After reviewing the evidence that prosperity, market institutions, and social modernization may themselves be doing the real work in the democracy-peace relationship, Hegre has the following section subhead: "Any Residual Effects of Democracy?"[11] Even if the direct effects of democracy on peace aren't zero, they're far from the whole story. And in the coming chapters, you'll see reform proposals designed to boost the socioeconomic development that is itself likely an important cause of greater peace. You shouldn't forget the democratic peace correlation, but digging into that correlation reminds us that there are many paths to peace.

Consider a recent paper coauthored by Hegre that dug deeper into the precise measures of national levels of democracy. The scholars reported that elections per se didn't seem to be the most crucial factor for predicting peace. Instead, "We find that the formal vertical channels of accountability provided by elections are not as crucial as horizontal constraint and the informal vertical accountability provided by a strong civil society."[12] So freer international trade, which has a tough time getting voter support, appears to raise the probability of peace, and elections likely aren't the most important factor for raising the probability of peace. Peace is important, but 10% less democracy isn't likely to detectably change the probability of peace, up or down.

Measuring Democracy

It's worth emphasizing that in this study, as in most other studies of the relationship between democracy on some societal outcome, researchers aren't using an all-or-nothing measure of democracy. Instead, they overwhelmingly use some form of score-based index, like the famed Polity IV index. The index, created by the Center for Systemic Peace in 1997 as the Polity index and updated over the decades, reports two major indexes: a Democracy index and a separate Autocracy index. The Democracy index measured from zero to ten combines three elements:

> One is the presence of institutions and procedures through which citizens can express effective preferences about alternative policies and leaders. Second is the existence of institutionalized constraints on the exercise of power by the executive. Third is the *guarantee of civil liberties to all citizens in their daily lives* [emphasis added] and in acts of political participation.[13]

Note the italics. This outcome-based measure of democracy comes naturally to many, but it's not part of Dahl's equal-political-participation definition of democracy. The Autocracy index by contrast focuses solely on the absence of vibrant, real-world political competition:

> In mature form, autocracies sharply restrict or suppress competitive political participation. Their chief executives are chosen in a regularized process of selection within the political elite, and once in office they exercise power with few institutional constraints. Most modern autocracies also exercise a high degree of directiveness over social and economic activity, but we regard this as a function of political ideology and choice, not a defining property of autocracy.[14]

The second sentence shows that the Polity IV team makes a distinction between the apparent correlates of autocracy (less freedom of social and economic choice) and autocracy itself (limited political competition). Many scholars follow the Polity IV's suggestion and just add those two indexes together to create an index of democracy. Other widely used measures exist as well, including the Freedom House democracy scores and the late Tatu Vanhanen's Index of Democratization. The Polity IV in particular is worth investigating online (it's available for free). The Polity IV team doesn't just drop rating numbers from the sky; instead, they offer a short essay on each country's political system, essays that are perhaps the equivalent of a democracy bond rating evaluation.

But note that the Polity IV's scores include more than just a measure of broad-based citizen involvement. To some degree, it blurs the distinction between citizen participation and civil rights in a way that is common in both scholarly and popular discussions of the merits of democracy. That means that on occasion, we'll have to keep an eye on whether "good policy outcomes" are being smuggled into the definition of democracy. Since I want to focus on whether slightly less voter involvement would improve or worsen government outcomes, that means I need to separate out measures of voter involvement from measures of government outcomes.

A Laffer Curve for Democracy?

In the 1980s, economist Art Laffer—then at the University of Southern California, now a professional economic consultant—drew a picture on a napkin that changed the world. As the legend goes, Laffer drew a simple graph with the horizontal axis labeled "Tax rate" and the vertical axis labeled "Tax revenue." On the graph, he drew a simple upside-down U: when the tax rate was zero, a government would raise no revenue, since it wasn't taxing anything. If the tax rate were 100%, again the government wouldn't raise any revenue, since people won't work or invest if they know government will take everything they earn—or, more realistically, people will shift to the underground, gray-market economy, working under the table and lying to the government about how much they really earn. At some point in the middle, there's a sweet spot—a tax rate that would maximize government revenue. And back in the United States of the

1970s, when the highest taxes rates reached 70%, Laffer was pretty sure that the tax rates were higher than the sweet spot: you could cut taxes and still bring in more government revenue.

These "bliss points" or sweet spots turn up again and again in a world of trade-offs. In evolution, there's a trade-off between the benefits of bigger size—you'll be stronger and so better able to catch prey—and the costs of bigger size—you'll need more calories each day, plus a bigger organism has more cells that can break down, plus you're an easier target for other predators to see. (It turns out that a strong rule in evolutionary biology is that larger mammal species have higher extinction rates. Tigers, elephants, and humans are relatively new, for instance, while the longest-lived mammal species include flying squirrels and a species of mole.[15]) Each species finds its own unique sweet spot—a balance between the benefits and costs of a bigger size. In economics, any time we see a relationship that can be summed up as an inverted U, we're pretty likely to call it a Laffer curve–type relationship, in homage to Art Laffer.

Fortunately, economists are well equipped to compare costs against benefits, but it means discarding the linear—or at least ordinal—thinking that is often the default setting in the social sciences. More democracy, more medical spending, more income per person, more human rights, more, more, more. If the current amount is good, why not have more? It's the buffet syndrome, an expression used in Singapore when people appear to overuse free government health care, so *buffet syndrome* means taking more with little regard to the cost.[16]

But as we'll see in the next nine chapters, voter involvement in government has not only benefits but costs—costs that are too often ignored. My contention is that the world's rich democracies are overall on the wrong side of the democracy Laffer curve, as Figure 1.1 suggests. Practical, nonutopian reforms exist that would:

- Make a country slightly less democratic
- Likely create substantial long-run economic benefits
- Have little or no cost in resources
- Be more likely to increase than to diminish widely embraced human rights.

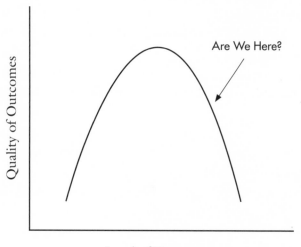

FIGURE 1.1. The Democracy Laffer Curve.

Just as important—for matters of practicality, if nothing else—countries that enacted these reforms would still look and feel and truly be democratic. After all, I'm not recommending 50% less democracy.

A Barrovian Parable

Two decades ago, Harvard economist Robert Barro published a fascinating set of papers, among the first to use then-new cross-country data to see which economic and social and geographic factors were good predictors of a nation's long-run economic performance. Barro ran multiple statistical horse races so one could tell which factors seemed more important and which were mere statistical illusions. One of the findings he trumpeted was that there appeared to be a Laffer curve relationship between democracy and long-run economic growth rates. At low levels of democracy, a bit more democracy predicted noticeably higher growth rates. Yet after a certain point, higher levels of democracy predicted noticeably slower growth rates. Barro estimated in 1996 that the democracy bliss point was at a fairly low level of democracy, and his forecasts are worth reflecting on: "The findings mean that growth would likely be reduced by further democratization in countries such as Mexico and Malaysia, which exhibit intermediate levels of the democracy indicator (0.5) in 1994. Moreover, future growth will probably be retarded by the political liberalizations that have already occurred in places such as Chile, Korea, and Taiwan."[17]

If Barro's Laffer curve theory of democracy were widely accepted in academic circles, my case would be halfway proven already. Beyond some point, there would be a clear democracy/prosperity trade-off, and while rich countries might indulge themselves by purchasing a high level of democracy, once citizens became aware of the cruel trade-off, once they became aware of the high economic price of higher voter involvement, they might be willing to dial voter power back just a bit.

I'll give a concrete illustration. In Barro's classic estimate, going from an average level of democracy to the highest levels was associated with 1.6% *lower* annual economic growth per person.[18] Over the course of a thirty-year generation, that would mean ending up about one-third poorer than a similar country that stuck with a medium level of democracy. Over three generations—the lives of our grandchildren—the miracle of compound growth means that the medium-democracy country would end up vastly richer than the high-democracy country. Would you be willing to support longer terms for politicians, tightened voter eligibility, and a single, hegemonic political party in exchange for a 300% raise? Well, *you* might not, but a lot of your neighbors probably would.

As it turns out, Barro's early Laffer curve results for democracy don't turn up in most of the more recent studies. More sophisticated methods—ones that can compare the same country before and after democratic reforms, for example—rarely yield the inverse-U relationship between democracy and growth. Instead, most studies find what I reported at the beginning of this chapter: a muddle, no clear relationship at all between a nation's degree of democracy and long-run economic performance.

This muddle means two things. First, it means that the popular folk belief that greater democracy *causes* better economic performance is just that—a folk belief, one without much serious minimum evidence on its behalf, at least once we are past the famine-avoiding level of democracy. Second, it means that since the data linking democracy and growth are in fact so noisy, so muddled, then these big overall comparisons aren't the way to evaluate the benefits and costs of a little more or a little less democracy. Instead, the way I'll make my case is by arguing for individual channels—precise mechanisms, precise policy reforms that by themselves are likely to yield big benefits at low (or lowish) costs.

I'll tie these claims to a plea: Although the overall relationship between democracy and economic performance appears muddled, as long as you're convinced that the precise democracy-reducing reforms that I suggest appear likely to work, I hope you'll give 10% less democracy a chance in the real world.

The Barrovian Precedent

This situation—a big-picture muddle that spurs us to dig deeper in search of ways to improve policy outcomes—isn't unique to the democracy and growth literature. In fact, Barro himself has contributed to this muddle in another area of research—in looking at the link between inflation and economic growth. As most card-carrying monetary economists like me can tell you, high inflation—a high average rate of growth in overall prices—is bad for the economy. Our textbooks detail the many ways inflation creates problems:

• Most real-world tax systems make you pay taxes on your interest earnings, even if almost all of that interest is just making up for high inflation.

• When inflation is high, it's usually unstable as well, so it's harder for people and businesses to make accurate long-run plans, which naturally depend on future prices.

• When inflation is high, people and businesses try to invest more of their wealth in safer assets that hold their value reliably over time, and so they divert wealth away from investing in possibly riskier, but socially more valuable, assets.

• Happiness surveys show that people really dislike inflation—not quite as much as unemployment, but it's not far off. One serious estimate based on happiness surveys run in the United States and Europe is that an extra 1% inflation reduces the average person's reported happiness as much as a 0.6% rise in the unemployment rate.[19]

• And it's just a hassle having to reevaluate the buying power of a dollar or a peso or a euro every few months. As Harvard's Greg Mankiw memorably put it, if we were holding a vote every year on how many inches should be in a foot, it's pretty obvious that every year, the winning option would always be "twelve inches."[20] If that's the case, why would we treat the buying power of a dollar any differently from the way we treat the measuring power of a ruler? Stable prices would mean we could spend our time thinking about more important issues.

So overall, the case for inflation rates that are very low or even zero seems pretty strong. Based on these tax, convenience, and investment-efficiency argument, it seems pretty hard to make a case that 7% annual inflation—the level the United States experienced in the 1970s—would be no big deal.

But here's the problem. When Barro himself checked—in an influential working paper originally published in the mid-1990s—to see if high inflation hurt long-run economic performance, using the same kind of cross-country comparisons widely used in the democracy-and-growth literature, he couldn't find any robust evidence that inflation hurt economic performance unless inflation was 15% or higher per year.[21] Below 15%, Barro couldn't rule out the possibility that inflation was hurting a nation's economic prospects, but the evidence was—that word again—a muddle. In the *Handbook of Economic Growth*, NYU's Easterly concluded in 2005, "The empirical literature on inflation has found that inflation only has a negative effect above some threshold level, although there are disagreements as to where that threshold is."[22]

What should a serious, candid, evidence-based thinker conclude? Does inflation hurt only when a nation is given a high, long-run dose of it? Is it economically irrelevant whether inflation is 1% per year versus 9% per year? No, it's not irrelevant; it's just that cross-country and decade-over-decade comparisons at the level of an entire nation can tell us only so much. And when these nation-level statistical techniques offer noisy and muddled testimony, it's best to turn to the testimony of precise, well-described channels—what economists call *microfoundations.*

Those microfoundations of the damaging effects of inflation— paying taxes on pure inflation gains, the hassle of printing new res- taurant menus every six months, the difficulty of making long-run business plans when you don't know whether inflation will be 4% or 12% next year- obviously add up to a sizable chunk of damage. Yes, 8% annual inflation is better than 80% annual inflation, but 8% a year, decade after decade, is still very likely causing long-run dam- age, even if nation-level statistical analysis can't confirm the damage. The microfounded evidence and arguments against inflation offer better, wiser, more useful information than the more ambiguous cross-country evidence.

And that's the approach I take in the coming chapters. Since the cross-country evidence about the relationship between democracy and economic performance is a giant "meh," I'll focus on precise, indi- vidual channels—microfoundations—to make the case that a little less democracy is good for the world's richest, most democratic nations.

The ABBA Approach to 10% Less Democracy: Take a Chance

Economists Benjamin Olken and Benjamin Jones (yes, they have the same first name) wrote an unusual paper comparing the economic outcomes of democracies to the economic outcomes of autocracies. They start off noting the usual—that once you compare apples with apples, autocracies grow at essentially the same rate as democracies on average. But they use that fact as a starting point, not an end- ing point. They wanted to test the traditional "great man" theory of history—that things really change (on average) when a nation's leader changes. To look for an answer, they investigate times when a political leader dies unexpectedly and then check to see what happened to the economy's growth rate over the next few years. The title of their paper asks the right question: *"Do leaders matter?"*[23]

They look at national economic performance after the surprise, nonassassination death of a political leader—and they note that heart disease is the most common cause of death in their sample. Does the death of a political leader change the nation's average economic growth rate? On average, no. But there's still a difference—and the difference is between what happens after the death of an autocratic leader and what happens after the death of a democratic leader. The big finding: if the nation is an autocracy, *growth volatility* rises massively after an assassination. When a dictator dies and a new leader takes over, the economy's growth rate might spike up or it might dive down, but it's not likely to keep growing at the same old rate. But when the leader of a democracy dies, nothing much tends to happen to the growth rate either way. The "leaders matter" theory seems to apply to autocracies much more than to democracies. Leaders matter a lot more when the top leader has more power.

You should keep the Olken and Jones finding in mind. Slightly reducing the level of democracy is risky; it's a slight move in the direction of autocracy. I'll be discussing reforms where the costs appear low, but they may not be zero. And all of these reforms have risks; they could turn out better than I suggest or worse. But I'm only recommending 10% less democracy for the world's richest democracies, not to countries at real risk of starvation or dictatorship.

Yes, the path to 10% less democracy has some risk. But on average, we're rich. We can afford to take some risk. We can take a chance.

2 Longer Terms, Braver Politicians

CAREER POLITICIANS ARE EXPERTS at getting reelected. In fact, the best short book on the U.S. Congress is built around that very idea. In *Congress: The Electoral Connection*, Yale political scientist David Mayhew argued that the best way to understand Congress is to think of it as a reelection factory.[1] The entire system—committees, chairmanships, hearings, votes—gives members plenty of opportunities to show their constituents back home that they are doing big things—plenty of opportunities to build a reputation as effective, dedicated, responsive representatives. You may think that Mayhew is just painting a cynical picture of politics today, but he was writing back in the 1970s. His story is a perennial one.

Under one view of democracy—the delegate view—this is actually a great outcome. Elected politicians in this view are delegated sovereign power by the voters to make the same decisions that the voters themselves would make if they had the time and energy to keep abreast of the key issues. It's a political version of the claim that the customer is always right. And one part of doing a great job representing your constituents is, well, letting your constituents know that you're doing a great job. Perhaps a little showmanship is just part of the price of government by the people. Perhaps the cost to society of all this showmanship is quite low.

But Mayhew's nearly anthropological analysis of Congress sug-gests otherwise. He was motivated in part by the work of my late George Mason University colleagues Jim Buchanan and Gordon Tullock, who pioneered the field now known as public choice. The public choice outlook treats politicians and voters largely the same way that economists treat firms and consumers: politicians want to maximize their chance of reelection just as firms want to maximize profits. Voters want political representatives who will give them the right bundle of goods and services at the lowest price, just as con-sumers want *their* preferred bundles of goods and services at the lowest price. Yes, there might be some altruistic politicians with noble motives, just as there might be profit-seeking corporations or nonprofits with noble motives—but in a competitive market, political or economic, it's safest to bet that altruism is rarely the biggest mo-tivator. An altruistic politician who decides not to run for reelection because she sees a better person in the running is about as rare as a carmaker telling customers, "Actually, the other guy's car is better and cheaper."

Driven to test the ideas of public choice theory, Mayhew showed how our political system itself creates dysfunction. When a politician has a choice between doing something where she can get public credit—like arranging funding for a Veterans Administration hospital expansion back in the home district—or doing something where she can't claim public credit—like investigating intelligence failures, where it's typically forbidden to publicly discuss committee work—a good politician doesn't take long to figure out that now is a good time to work on those hospital expansions. The system encourages politicians to work on projects where it's easier and more credible to publicly claim credit.

And it's important to make those claims of credit credible. Because of the way Congress is set up, voters are skeptical when a politician claims that she's getting a lot done. It's easy to just tell people you're doing a great job, but talk is cheap. It's harder to really prove it—and politicians take this into account when choosing their goals. That means voters put more weight on visible outcomes—pork projects like a new highway interchange or that Veterans Affairs hospital expansion—and less weight on invisible outcomes—working hard on the House Intelligence Committee, where you're dealing with government secrets and can't really tell anyone what you do all day. Voters like it when politicians bring home the bacon, but not just because extra school funding or new jobs at the military base are great on their own. Voters also like it because pork is a decent signal that a politician isn't just spending time at fundraisers. Pork proves that the politician did at least some work on behalf of regular voters. Alas, that means elected politicians will focus too much on the visible and too little on the invisible. And if there's one great and wise lesson of economic thinking, it's French economist Frédéric Bastiat's from 1848: "There is only one difference between a bad economist and a good one: the bad economist confines himself to the visible effect; the good economist takes into account both the effect that can be seen and those effects that must be foreseen."[2]

So better economic policy choices are possible if there's some social mechanism, some invisible hand, that spurs politicians to give real attention to invisible effects, effects that are unseen today but potentially foreseen. This chapter points toward such a mechanism— and it relies on voter forgetfulness.

Backloading the Pork: A Sign of Voter Amnesia

The theory that voters want to see visible results while, simultaneously, politicians try to provide voters with those visible results has been tested more formally and less anthropologically. Decades after Mayhew's book, Harvard political scientist Kenneth Shepsle and his coauthors used Mayhew's ideas to demonstrate that voters have short memories. And since voters have short memories, the political system focuses on pleasing them in the near term.

As I noted in the Introduction, U.S. senators hold six-year terms and are always eligible to run for reelection; there are no term limits. That means that once a senator gets elected, she has six years to build a reputation and make a good impression on the voters back home. But as Shepsle found, senators instead tend to backload the pork, delivering 15% more projects and 15% more dollars in home-state spending in the last two years of their cycle, so the biggest payoff happens just when the senator is in cycle.[3] A senator acts like a teenager who wants to borrow the family car for senior prom: he starts cleaning up his bedroom a couple of days before the big ask. And the fact that this works—on voters and on parents—is a sign that most of us pay too much attention to the recent past.

"What have you done for me lately?" isn't just a fantastic Janet Jackson hit from the 1980s; for many, it's the standard question when evaluating others. We see this focus on recent rewards in other settings, as in the debate over whether American corporations are too focused on meeting quarterly profit expectations. Why can't companies focus on the long run, on making big strategic decisions that might not pay off for years? Doesn't that shortsighted focus on the last three months of profits weaken long-run corporate performance? It probably does, and the same lesson is at work in the U.S. Senate: if voters are as shortsighted as some say stock watchers are, that's going to hurt our nation's economic, social, and foreign policy performance.

More evidence on voter shortsightedness comes from Yale economist Ray Fair, renowned as an economic forecaster. His model for predicting U.S. presidential vote outcomes uses data going back a century—his sample begins in 1916. He found that the election-year economy mattered a lot to those deciding whom to support for president. In 2009 he summed up his key measure of economic growth: "the growth rate . . . of real per capita GDP in the first three quarters of the election year."[4]

Real per capita GDP is inflation-adjusted income per person. And three quarters—the first nine months of the election year—is what voters appear to care about when choosing the president. That's right. For the purpose of choosing the leader of the free world, the American voter's memory of income growth doesn't go back more than a year.

Two caveats. First, Fair did update his model in the early 1990s after George H. W. Bush lost despite lackluster but not abysmal economic performance. Afterward, Fair found that voters do seem to recall economic outcomes going back further than the election year if the economic news was extremely good—if there were "boom quarters." So voters might remember extremes from the distant past of two or three years ago, and that's worth keeping in mind. But such boom quarters are atypical—and if voters can recall old news only if it's wildly exceptional, that is itself a sign we should be at least a little reluctant to trust voters with our long-run economic future. Furthermore, Fair's forecasting model suggests that there's more noise in the boom quarter effect than in the election year growth effect.[5] The second caveat is that voters remember and hate high inflation, even if it happened back at the start of the presidential term. But when it comes to classic pocketbook issues, to real income growth, the economic effect of presidential elections typically and most robustly turns on the extremely recent past.

An optimist might retort that perhaps short-term memories are a blessing in disguise. Perhaps a senator will make good, tough, farsighted decisions that would be unpopular with voters when the election is four or five years out, pandering only when he's "in cycle," a year or two away from a reelection bid. Perhaps it's also possible that senators just pander to a different crowd—to donors—for the first four years and then pivot to voters for the last two. Maybe it's a mixed bag. Verbal theorizing can't answer this question for us, but recent data-driven research can help us sort this out.

Short Terms Cause Short-Term Thinking

> The evidence on official term length suggests that very short terms
> do not seem to be favorable.
>
> Mark Schelker

When it comes to international trade, economists are about as uni-fied in their views as any group of experts can be. The University of Chicago's Initiative on Global Markets (IGM) regularly sur-veys both leading economists around the world, as well as a sepa-rate European-focused group of economists on a variety of policy questions. Regardless of how the questions have been phrased in the past decade, both the global IGM panel and the European IGM panel have overwhelmingly agreed that reducing trade barriers is good for the nation that lowers them. Letting foreigners compete in your markets is good for you, partly because you get cheaper goods and partly because the invisible hand will move your nation's workers over to more productive uses.

Here's a statement from 2016 that the IGM's economists were asked to disagree or agree with: "Freer movement of goods and services across borders within Europe has made the average western European citizen better off since the 1980s."[6] Of the European economists surveyed, 68% strongly agreed and another 24% agreed—just about everybody. And since economists routinely consider how trade changes the income distribution, the IGM European panel was asked to disagree or agree with this statement: "Freer movement of goods and services across borders within Europe has made many low-skilled western European citizens worse off since the 1980s." Here there was more disagreement: 20% agreed that lower-skilled citizens were often worse off, and 2% more strongly agreed, while 42% disagreed and 10% strongly disagreed. The uncertain were 18% of the sample. That means about one in five thought many lower-skilled workers were worse off, and another one in five weren't sure. But there's nothing close to a consensus that intra-Europe trade deals hurt lower-skilled Western European citizens. Pie-growing change often entails real costs, of course, and they're not always the kind of costs you can measure with money. When the family moves to a big city so the parents can earn more, there's probably one kid in the family who loses a treasured best friend, never to be regained.

A 2018 survey about European trade with China yielded similar answers: freer trade with China appeared great for Europeans, and while it certainly hurt European workers (as workers) in key industries, that alone wasn't sufficient to argue for a policy like higher import taxes on imported Chinese steel.[7]

With high rates of agreement on the overall benefits of low trade barriers, economists agree with each other to approximately the same extent that physicians agree on HPV vaccination for teenage girls, with approval rates of around 90%.[8] That's a near consensus of experts.

So what makes politicians more likely to support the expert consensus? For some answers, let's turn to evidence from the U.S. Congress. While senators have six year terms, members of the lower house of the legislature, the U.S. House of Representatives, have just two-year terms. What encourages senators to vote for lower trade barriers? One big factor is being years away from reelection. When a senator is in cycle, she's 10 percentage points less likely to vote for a trade deal. Economist Paola Conconi of the Université Libre de Bruxelles and her coauthors established this fact in an aptly titled paper published in 2014: "Policymakers' Horizon and Trade Reforms: The Protectionist Effect of Elections." They provide anecdotal evidence for their case in a footnote: "For example, during her first [term] as senator from New York state, Hillary Clinton voted on six trade liberalization bills, four times in favor (during the first four years) and twice against (during the last two years)."[9] Politicians act differently when the election looms. They don't just show up to more county fairs and church services; they also are more reluctant to support one policy reform that experts overwhelmingly agree on: freer international trade.

Conconi reports another important finding: senators who are in cycle act just like House members. A senator who is in cycle is just as likely to vote for a trade deal as a member of the more protectionist U.S. House of Representatives, where everyone is always less than two years away from reelection. And finally, senators who are in safe seats or are retiring vote just like senators who aren't in cycle: the protectionist effect of elections "disappears for senators who are not afraid of losing office."[10] A looming election—especially a potentially close election—focuses the mind on the protectionist attitudes of voters.

Conconi's creative study packs a lot of power because it compares in-cycle senators to three very different groups—out-of-cycle senators, House members, and in-cycle senators who don't fear the voters—and yields consistent results: when elections are looming and expected to be tight, U.S. politicians are less likely to support a policy that most economists would support. In a later study, economist Paola Coconi and coauthors found that U.S. presidents are more likely to file trade dispute grievances just before a presidential election. The title of their paper says it all: "Suspiciously Timed Trade Disputes." Even better, they report just how good presidents are at focusing on the political consequences of these trade disputes: "Moreover, U.S. trade disputes are more likely to involve industries that are important in swing states."[11]

It's politics all the way down, and short-term, swing-state politics at that. Calm and cool planning for the economy's long-run prosperity this is not. It appears from decades of data and across dozens of decisions that looming elections are bad news for good economics.[12]

Looming Elections the World Over

This isn't a story that applies just to the United States, however. On average, this story holds around the world. The best evidence comes from a study of International Monetary Fund (IMF) programs coauthored by Stephanie Rickard of the London School of Economics and Teri Caraway of the University of Minnesota, both professors of government.[13] The IMF's loan and aid packages to developing economies often come with strings attached. One set of strings is labor market reforms: demands that a nation lower the minimum wage, make it easier to fire workers, and make other, related changes that many citizens will oppose. As with international trade policy, labor market policy is an area where economists tend to agree with each other and tend to disagree with the general public. The IGM's European panel responded to this statement in 2017 when French president Emmanuel Macron was proposing substantial labor market reforms: "Revising France's labor market policies—by reducing employment protection, decentralizing labor negotiations to the firm level, and making training programs more accessible and responsive to labor demands—would, all else equal, increase productivity in France's economy."[14] They also responded to, "Reducing employment protection would reduce the equilibrium unemployment rate in France."

"Productivity" means output per worker, so the statement is a claim about whether the reforms would increase the size of the pie. The second statement is closer to a question about whether the reforms would help those lower in the economic spectrum, since high unemployment rates in Europe tend to hurt those with less human capital and experience. On the productivity statement, two-thirds agreed or strongly agreed, and on unemployment rates, half agreed and many abstained or were uncertain, but in neither case did more than 5% of respondents disagree with the statement.[15] The economists' consensus on labor market reforms isn't as overwhelming as with trade liberalization, but almost all the weight is on one side—the side of market-friendly, liberal economics.

So how do looming elections fit into this? Rickard and Caraway checked to see if the IMF imposed fewer labor market liberalization reforms when an election was looming. Financial crises are somewhat random, so if they happen when elections are years away, does the IMF demand lots of pie-growing, productivity-increasing reforms? Rickard and Caraway report, drawing on 297 IMF interventions in democracies the world over, "Labor conditions included in programs signed within six months of an upcoming election are, on average, 50 percent less stringent than those in loans agreed more than six months away from elections."[16] It turns out the IMF behaves a lot like many U.S. senators: when an election looms, it's reluctant to push for reforms that are relatively popular with experts but unpopular with voters.

Another set of studies finds that nations facing financial trouble are reluctant to take one useful dose of medicine: weakening the nation's exchange rate, devaluing the currency. Jeffry Frieden of Harvard's Department of Government is a leading contributor in this area. In a 2001 paper focusing on Latin America, he and his coauthors note, "Devaluations tend to be delayed in the run-up to elections, and only occur immediately after the new government takes office."[17]

A currency devaluation tends to boost exports by making exports cheaper for foreigners to buy (which directly helps export-driven industries, a small but important and frequently highly productive part of the economy); it also makes imports more expensive (which tends to hurt consumers if they're buying a lot of goods like smartphones, televisions, and other imported electronics). Again, voters are probably going to be unhappy about a devaluation in the short run, even if it's a practical way to strengthen the nation's economy. As Mareike Kleine and Clement Minaudier, both of the London School of Economics, sum it up, "Frieden, Ghezzi and Stein find that governments shy away from undertaking corrective but potentially unpopular devaluations right before national elections."[18]

So now we have three major areas where governments facing a looming election are reluctant to take the tough but probably effective medicine: trade policy, labor regulation, and exchange rate policy. It appears that when voters are watching, political elites are reluctant to increase the size of the economic pie.

"Nothing Gets Done in Election Years"

So far, we've focused on the tendency to make popular calls—or sidestep unpopular ones—as elections draw near. But there's another effect of looming elections that comes up more often in political discussions: the fact that it's hard to get anything done during an election year. Studying democratic Argentina, Eduardo Alemán and Ernesto Calvo of the University of Houston report that the national legislature holds fewer sessions during election years, at least in part because it's hard to get a large enough group—a quorum—to do business.[19] That might not be all bad; indeed there might be quite a lot of good that comes from having legislatures and executives out there campaigning if the alternative is passing bad laws.

However, low legislative productivity in election years is no demo-cratic universal. Frank Baumgartner of the University of North Caro-lina and coauthors report that French legislators do fit the pattern of low productivity in election years and are substantially less likely to pass either mundane bills or major policy changes in election years. But in the United States, where major elections are held every two years, Baumgartner reports that legislators tend to hold more hear-ings the first year of the two-year cycle and then pass more bills in the second year, the election year. But even in the United States, there's a noteworthy pattern: although Congress passes around 50% more bills overall in election years, the major policy bills are spread almost evenly across the two-year cycle. That means that *in relative terms,* politicians are pulling the tougher decisions forward in time—to the first year of the two-year cycle—and pushing tough decisions away from the looming election. In an important sense, then, legislators in Argentina, France, and the United States are doing relatively more of the substantive work early in the legislative term.[20]

Let's take a moment to look at an unconventional piece of evi-dence that less gets done in the halls of government during election season. A study of European Union countries from 1976 through 2009 found that when EU member nations have elections in the near future, the EU's government in Brussels is less likely to enact agree-ments. It's not just that, say, German elections slow down legislation in Germany; it's that German elections slow down legislation for the entire EU. The authors, Kleine and Minaudier of the London School of Economics, find that "the chances of reaching an agreement are significantly reduced when a national election is pending, and that this effect is especially pronounced in the case of close elections in large member states."[21]

A final, quite unusual piece of evidence that longer terms get poli-ticians to work harder comes from a study coauthored by Berkeley economist Ernesto Dal Bó and economist Martin Rossi of Argentina's University of San Andres.[22] The team looked at two political reforms in Argentina that randomly lengthened the terms of some politicians, and then they checked to see how that changed the behavior of those politicians compared to both the recent past and other politicians who hadn't had their terms lengthened at random. The Argentine government did this twice: once in the House of Representatives in 1983, switching to two- and four-year terms, and in 2001 in the Senate, switching to two-, four-, and six-year terms. The randomization was apparently real: on a certain date, the government held a public lottery draw. The research team measured "legislative effort" in a few ways: bills submitted by a particular legislator, bills submitted by that legislator that eventually became law, and four other similarly objective measures. The authors summarize one of their findings: "For example, longer terms increase senatorial bill submissions by almost 50%, and for representatives, they almost double the number of bills that get approved."[23] They conclude that

> longer terms increase effort. Shorter terms appear to discourage effort not due to campaign distractions but due to an investment payback logic: when effort yields returns over multiple periods, longer terms yield a higher chance of capturing those returns. A broader implication is that job stability may promote effort despite making individuals less accountable.[24]

And then Bó and Rossi do something that my fellow economists do infrequently but should do more often: they actually talked to the legislators themselves and asked them how longer terms changed their own incentives. Of course, politicians, like CEOs and spouses, have an incentive to put the best foot forward, but their thoughts are still well worth a listen. When the politicians were asked whether the promise of job stability spurred them to put more effort into being good legislators, they "rated this explanation as highly plausible."[25]

Political scientist Rocío Titiunik of the University of Michigan found something similar when she looked at U.S. state senators. When state legislative districts were redrawn within Arkansas, Illinois, and Texas, some state senators were randomly assigned to two- or four-year terms. This natural experiment lets us know something about causation, not just correlation. Titiunik's title captures this: "Drawing Your Senator from a Jar: Term Length and Legislative Behavior." From the abstract:

> Despite important differences across states, when considered to-gether, the results show that senators serving two years abstain more often, introduce fewer bills, and do not seem to be more responsive to their constituents than senators serving four years. In addition, senators serving shorter terms raise and spend signifi-cantly more money.[26]

While it isn't impossible that the relative sloth of these two-year legislators is optimal, it's safer to bet against that option. Politi-cians have a lot of different ways to spend their time, among them campaigning, working on legislation, meeting with celebrities, or building networks to try to get a future job as a corporate lobbyist. Getting politicians to actually work at all on legislation is apparently relatively hard, and as we've repeatedly seen, getting politicians to take tough votes that please the experts more than the masses is probably even harder. Frequent elections shrink the supply of legisla-tion overall; more important, they likely shrink the supply of some good legislation.

Politicians have limits to their bravery, and an election year isn't the best time to ask an elected official to turn down the demands of the voters. But democracies require frequent elections—one of Robert Dahl's requirements for democracy in *On Democracy* is that elections be "free, fair, and frequent"—and the longer the term, the less often the voters have a voice in government.[27] Of course, frequency is a matter of degree: twenty-year terms would be quite undemocratic, while the annual terms common in ancient Athens ensured that the voting citizens could keep close control over state power. Shorter term lengths are one tool for citizen control of the state, one tool for rule by the people.

If elections were a little less frequent—for instance, if po-litical terms of two or three years were lengthened to four or six years—politicians would find bravery a little easier to come by, the world's rich democracies would stand a better chance of getting better economic policies, and we'd all still feel like we lived in democracies. This is the kind of reform proposal you'll see more of in the coming chapters: a change that pulls a small amount of power away from voters but still gives citizens an important voice in government. That's what 10% less democracy should look like.

3 Central Bank "Independence"

THE POWER TO PRINT MONEY — and to then decide who gets that money—has to be on the top ten list of superpowers. It's clearly way ahead of heat vision or clinging to walls, but unlike the superpowers you read about in comic books, the power to print money actually exists. And it's a power that the rich democracies have overwhelmingly kept about as far away from voters as humanly possible.

Central banks—like the European Central Bank, the Bank of Japan, the Bank of England, and the U.S. Federal Reserve (the Fed)—are the government entities that are typically granted this power. Central banks today mostly do their job by "lending" money to other banks, but the money they lend is different from the money that you lend. When you want to lend money, you have to find the money before you lend it out, but when a central bank wants to lend money, it just . . . well, it just creates it out of thin air. It's typically created as an electronic credit deposited to the account of, say, Deutsche Bank. Once it's been created and deposited to that private bank's account, that private bank can go and spend the money more or less as it will—though typically its goal is to lend that money out as quickly as possible at a higher interest rate. If it doesn't repay the loan it received from the central bank on time, it'll typically get into big trouble, so it's genuinely not free money from Deutsche Bank's point of view—*but it was free for the central bank to create the money in the first place.*

Central banks do a lot more than that, of course, but that's their classic job: lend money on generous terms (say, low interest rates) when the central bank wants to give the economy a boost, or lend money on tougher terms (at higher interest rates) when the central bank wants to slow things down a bit. One can spend a lifetime on the details—my dissertation was about just one tiny detail, how the Federal Reserve controls interest rates on a day-to-day basis—but that's the core channel.

The power to print money is the core power granted to central banks, and it's a power that European, Japanese, British, and American governments have kept far from the hands of voters. That antidemocratic decision has typically been seen as a great choice according to mainstream economists, and in this chapter we'll see just why that is. By looking in detail at the case of central banks, we'll build both a case for greater elite control of some parts of government and a critique of citizen control of those same parts of government.

Undemocratic Central Banks: A Free Lunch?

"There's no such thing as a free lunch." That's a saying I've heard for decades, and we economists love to repeat it. It captures our professional cynicism and our need to remind ourselves that life is full of difficult trade-offs. But what if there really is a free lunch, and what if it's both delicious and nutritious? My professional advice, as a wildly overtrained economist, is that you should eat the free lunch.

In 1993, two Harvard economists reported an amazing free lunch, but it came with a hitch: to eat it, you had to sacrifice just a little bit of democracy. Alberto Alesina and Larry Summers asked a classic question: Should a nation's central bank be under the direct control of a nation's elected officials?[1] Or should it instead be independent of the elected officials, out of touch with the fickle mood of the voters and instead more like judges appointed for life? And they measured the goals of a central bank quite reasonably. If possible, the central bank should aim for low, stable inflation; a low, stable unemployment rate; and a fast, stable rate of economic growth. Fairly stable prices and fairly abundant jobs: as policy goals go, relatively uncontroversial.

Which kind of central bank could come closest to accomplishing these goals: the politically connected ones or the out-of-touch ones? Before we turn to their answer, we should first consider the possibility that the question is simply ill posed. Maybe there really is no free lunch, and maybe having more of one item on the menu means getting less of another. Maybe if my team gets more, your team gets less.

That outcome can't be dismissed: it has a long tradition in economic thought, both technical and popular. Maybe, as then-future Nobel laureates Paul Samuelson and Robert Solow of MIT and James Tobin of Yale had suggested in the 1960s, there was some kind of near-permanent trade-off between low inflation and low unemployment. The government could choose to help out workers by heating up the economy, creating persistently low unemployment at the cost of persistently higher inflation, or it could instead help out the financial class, people with savings accounts and bonds, by keeping a cooler economy with lower inflation at the cost of higher unemployment. In 1965 Tobin applied this trade-off to the United States, in a volume for which Vice President Lyndon Johnson wrote the Foreword:

> We know how to operate the economy so that there is a tight labor market. By fiscal and monetary measures the federal government can control aggregate spending in the economy. The government could choose to control it so that unemployment *averaged* 3.5 or 3 per cent instead of remaining over 4.5 percent. . . . Running the economy with a tight labor market would mean a somewhat faster upward creep in the price level.[2]

So in the 1960s MIT view, lower average unemployment would come at the cost of higher average inflation—a classic cruel trade-off, a lunch with a price tag.

Other future Nobel laureates, including the University of Chicago's Milton Friedman and Robert Lucas and the University of Minnesota's Thomas Sargent, had written in the 1960s (Friedman) and 1970s (Lucas and Sargent) that there really *was* no cruel trade-off, no hidden class warfare in the decisions of central banking policy. They argued instead that the economy could adjust to any inflation rate relatively well after some adjustment period. These so-called freshwater economists (so-called because their universities were near the American Great Lakes, to distinguish them from the "saltwater" economists near Boston) differed among each other about the optimal inflation rate, but they didn't think that a high inflation rate went hand in hand with lower unemployment. If anything, they were more likely to believe the opposite: that times of high inflation were times of economic disruption and thus higher unemployment, and so the inflation was itself a symptom of trouble elsewhere in the economy.

Thus, the question of the right kind of central bank was intimately connected with the question of how the overall economy worked. Did monetary policy involve cruel trade-offs, or did it involve free lunches? And once one answered the question of how the economy actually worked, one could then turn to the question of which type of central bank was best at making good monetary policy decisions: one run directly by politicians or one run by independent appointees.

Let's now turn to that second question. It was only in the early 1980s that economists Michael Bade and Michael Parkin, both of the University of Western Ontario, started to collect data that could answer the question with systematic facts rather than with theory and anecdote. They and others used a simple method to measure what they euphemistically called "central bank independence" (CBI). The most basic measure of CBI was whether the head of the central bank could be fired by the nation's top political leader. If the prime minister or president gets upset with the head of the central bank, could he fire her just like he would a defense minister or a White House chief of staff? If not—if the central bank president had something like tenure—then that was one sign that the central bank was somewhat independent of the political system.

Harvard's Alesina and Summers note that CBI is typically broken down into "political independence" and "economic independence." They summarize political independence:

> Whether or not its governor and the board are appointed by the government, the length of their appointments [longer is more independent], whether government representatives sit on the board of the bank [a bad sign], whether government approval for monetary policy decisions is required [another bad sign] and whether the "price stability" objective is explicitly and prominently part of the central bank statute [a good sign—a sign of focus].[3]

Economic independence is different: it measures whether the central bank is permitted to say "No!" to the government. After all, many nations have been ruined by governments that forced the central bank to lend the government money on easy terms, setting off inflationary and even hyperinflationary spirals. Alesina and Summers's summary of economic independence:

> The ability to use instruments of monetary policy without restrictions. The most common constraint imposed upon the conduct of monetary policy is the extent to which the central bank is required to finance [the] government deficit.[4]

Think of an economically independent central bank as one that is free to ignore the government's requests for cheap money.

The early CBI work focused on the same countries this book does: the relatively prosperous countries, mostly in Western Europe, North America, and East Asia. And the first figure Alesina and Summers present is the same one reprinted in economics textbooks around the world to make the point that politics—democratic politics—gets in the way of good monetary policy.

Figure 3.1 shows how independent, generally less democratic central banks—those on the right side of the figure like Switzerland, Germany, and the United States—averaged 4% lower long-run rates

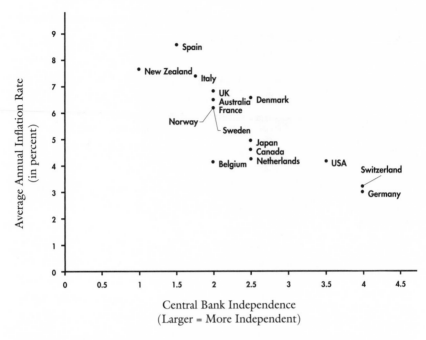

FIGURE 3.1. Central Bank Independence and Inflation: A Negative Relationship. Source: Alesina and Summers (1993).

of annual inflation compared to countries with the most politician-dependent central banks—those on the left side, New Zealand and Spain. If, as neoclassical Nobel-winning economists like Lucas, Sargent, and Friedman said, the main job of a central bank is to maintain a low average rate of inflation, then it's clear that the politically disconnected central banks are the ones that are getting the job done.

Of course, any time you see data plotted out like this, with a strong correlation like this one, you should remind yourself that correlation isn't causation—that having a chandelier in your house doesn't make you rich (even though it's a sign you're rich), that buying a baby stroller won't make you a parent (though it's a sign a baby is on the way). But then what *is* causation? How can we know whether it's the legal independence of the central banks of the United States, Switzerland, and Germany that is getting the job done? For instance, maybe instead it's "German culture" that makes German inflation low. The classic story, after all, is that the post–World War II German collective memory of the 1920s hyperinflation created a culture that demanded low inflation after the war.

And so perhaps an alternate explanation might go that German postwar culture was so insistent on low inflation that Germans bought all the bells and whistles that were supposed to go along with low inflation, including an independent central bank. Sure, an independent central bank probably doesn't hurt, but maybe it's not in the driver's seat. Maybe it's the citizen demand for good monetary policy that helps produce good monetary policy—so maybe democracy really is running the monetary policy show behind the scenes.

One informal way to test the theory that CBI matters by itself is to see what happens when a new political party comes to power and quickly changes how the central bank does its job. So before turning to more cross-country statistics, let's look at an anecdotal test: the case of New Zealand. In 1989, the country that had had the most politician-dependent central bank in the Alesina-Summers paper switched its central banking policy completely. Within months, the Reserve Bank of New Zealand went from the left side of Figure 3.1 to the right side, from low CBI to high CBI. By 1991 New Zealand's inflation rate, which had averaged well over 10% per year for most of the 1970s and 1980s—a substantially higher rate than the United States experienced during its "Great Inflation" of the 1970s—was down to 1% per year. New Zealand's inflation has averaged about 2% per year ever since. Inflation there has stayed low even as partisan coalitions left and right have formed and broken apart. When New Zealand's politicians decided to hand over power to an unelected central bank, that decision turned out to last and to matter.

Fancier cross-country statistical evidence confirms that this is a pattern: when countries increase the independence of their central banks, the inflation rate tends to fall. That's what Australian economists Alberto Posso and George Tawadros report after looking at dozens of countries across the past few decades.[5] As economic relationships go, this is a robust one: when politicians get out of the banking business, inflation falls. This isn't evidence that just comes from comparing one country against another as in Figure 3.1: the same evidence shows up when we compare the same country against itself as it goes from politician-run to insider-run central banks.

So more apparently, CBI cuts inflation. But what if inflation falls at the price of higher unemployment? What if the national economy really is a battle between the financial class and the working class, as Yale's Tobin had suggested, and what if independent central banks are just funneling more economic weapons to financial elites? That's where the next two graphs, Figures 3.2 and 3.3, based on the 1993 Alesina and Summers paper, come in. Countries with more independent, less democratic central banks had just about the same rates of unemployment and just about the same growth rate of income per person as countries with heavily political central banks.

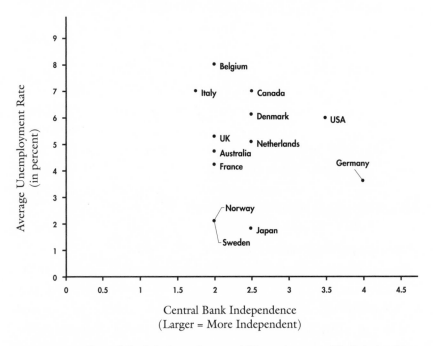

FIGURE 3.2. Central Bank Independence and Unemployment: No Relationship. Source: Alesina and Summers (1993).

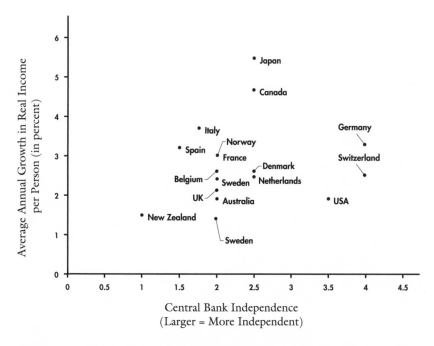

FIGURE 3.3. Central Bank Independence and Income Growth: No Relationship. Source: Alesina and Summers (1993).

The volatility graphs (omitted here) tell the same story: inflation is less volatile, and economic growth and unemployment are no more volatile and probably a bit less volatile, in countries with independent central banks. Overall, independent central banks look like a free lunch. The only thing you have to lose is your high inflation—and your president's right to fire the central bank president.

Simple Data, Deep Insights

Other economists, especially Alex Cukierman of Tel Aviv University and Princeton, and Vittorio Grilli, Donato Masciandaro, and Guido Tabellini, whose careers span London, Milan, and Los Angeles, respectively, had been measuring the merits of independent central banks, but it was the Alesina and Summers paper that created a revolution.[6] I suspect it was a combination of factors that made this the paper that took off. It didn't hurt that it was written by two Harvard professors, that it was published in the excellent *Journal of Money, Credit, and Banking*, and that the authors already had great reputations at young ages of writing fun, interesting, important papers.

But there was more than that. This was a world-changing paper with zero fancy statistics. It had only the raw scatter plots you see here, and the appendixes reported the raw numbers so anyone could use the data themselves. None of the high-powered calculus, probability theory, or statistical formulas that economists study in graduate school appear in the paper. Indeed the authors spend little time addressing the "Well, whatabouts": Well, what about the possibility that Switzerland is just naturally a low inflation country? Or what about the possibility that Catholic countries tend to have a little more corruption and maybe that's why they have higher inflation? You can imagine such questions could go on endlessly—I hinted at that already with the German case—and questions like this have continued for decades.

But sometimes it just seems obvious what's going on, and it's good to make your case clearly. Alesina and Summers were pretty sure why politically detached central banks were good for the economy, and they wanted to get other people to debate them about it. With a hint of self-deprecation, they note, "We have looked at the data only in a very straightforward way; more detailed analysis of the relation between central bank independence and real performance is warranted."[7]

The more detailed analysis has continued, and it's safe to say that Alesina and Summers's preferred explanation is still a big part of the story: "Our findings . . . have implications for the ongoing debate over the optimal rules governing monetary policy. Most obviously they suggest the economic performance merits of central bank independence."[8]

The Written Rules Versus the Real Rules

The early central bank research looked at formal, written rules to see if central banks were independent: How long is the term of the president? Is the finance minister a member of the central bank's board? But in real life, we all know that there's often a chasm between the written rules and the real rules. Sometimes a phone call from the finance minister can change half the votes on the central bank board, even if the finance minister has no official power over that bank. So within a few years, economists started looking for proxies of genuine central bank independence. Two worth mentioning are how long central bank board members stay on the board (longer means more independence) and how often central bank board members step down after the politician who appointed them leaves office (if you leave when your benefactor leaves, that's a sign your true power depends on the politician who appointed you).[9]

It turns out that in rich countries with good political systems—countries that tend to have relatively low corruption and strong political institutions—the written rules and the real rules tell pretty much the same story. Both long *statutory* terms and low *real-world* turnover on the central bank board predict lower inflation. But in poorer countries, those with higher corruption levels and weaker institutions, the real rules (actual term length and whether you quit when your benefactor quits) are far better predictors of economic outcomes.

Occasionally my fellow economists are derided as naive, out-of-touch scholars who know little and care less about how the real world works. But the central bank independence literature is just one example of how my fellow economists have kicked the tires and looked under the hood of their own findings. Part of the reason Cukierman and others did that is because economists know that other economists are a tough, skeptical audience. In our profession, we pass around stories of economists giving seminars on their research papers—usually at the University of Chicago, home to more Nobel laureates in economics than any other university—and never getting more than ten minutes into their slides because the other professors in the room tear the paper apart piece by piece for the next ninety minutes. The fear that such a prospect creates in the human heart spurs us to strengthen our arguments, find the data, check and see if we're actually correct or if we're just living in a dream world of our own creation.

I'm taking that approach here, though in a nontechnical way: noting that multiple kinds of evidence, multiple measures of central bank independence, point toward the same prediction. The less political, the less democratic, the more insider driven the nation's central bank is, the better the outcomes. A bundle of correlations tied together with some suggestions of causation.

Oh, and here's a small bonus in this tire-kicking line of research. Cukierman, like others, doesn't find any noticeable evidence from the rich countries that central bank independence makes your country richer. You get lower, more stable inflation (which voters love), plus a more stable unemployment rate and a more stable economy overall, and those are great benefits. But in the middle- and lower-income countries, it appears—at least in his data—that you get something more: If your central bank is more independent, your economy grows a little bit faster, so your nation gets richer in the long run. When looking at data from poorer countries in the 1960s, 1970s, and 1980s, Cukierman and his coauthors found that even if you knew about changes in the price of a nation's exports, its education level, and how rich the country was at the time, you could still do a better job predicting how fast the economy would grow in the future if you knew these real-world measures of central bank independence. You may even get a higher rate of investment in machines and equipment—physical capital—though that's more speculative. But overall, it's easy to find evidence for the theory that getting central banking out of the hands of politicians (and voters!) is pretty much a win all around.

Working in Theory

Old joke: An economist is someone who, after seeing something work in practice, asks, "But does it work in theory?" The fact is now there, and it's pretty robust: less democratic central banks work in practice. But why? That's the question we'll turn to here, and abstract, unrealistic economic theory will do a lot of the heavy lifting.

This step is important because finding out the sources of the strengths of independent central banks will likely give us hints about the weaknesses of democracy. If we can find out why modern representative democracy does an awful job running a nation's monetary policy, we might get a sense of which other tasks might be especially ill suited to voter control.

One theory goes like this. Let's pretend you're a politician. Even if you, the politician, care deeply about increasing job growth and even if you'd be personally tempted to badger the central bank to go on lending sprees to help the economy (especially just before an election!), you're still better off if you delegated the job of running monetary policy to a "conservative central banker," one who only cares about a low, stable inflation rate and doesn't care at all about the unemployment rate. This theory, created by former chess champion and current Harvard economist Kenneth Rogoff, goes something like this . . . [10]

The Conservative Central Banker: An Origin Story

The only way to use monetary policy to boost the real economy is to surprise the citizens with cheap money. The cheap money gets people more spending and creates more jobs in the short run (before prices rise). But then eventually prices rise, goods don't feel cheap any more, and the boom ends.

But you can't surprise the citizens that often. Eventually (and perhaps even immediately) they catch on, and so as soon as the money gets plentiful, businesses raise their prices and workers raise their wage demands. With both goods and workers getting more expensive, you get a boom in prices and wages but no boom in real output, no boom in jobs. All hangover, no buzz.

Since a hangover without a preceding buzz is a pure waste and since this model (and our reality) depends on tricking people with temporary cheap money, and since Abraham Lincoln was right when he (according to poorly substantiated legend) said you can't fool all of the people all of the time, it's a bad idea to try to fool the voters with cheap money. Alas, while trying to fool the voters is a bad idea, both the voters and the government know that the government is sorely tempted to print cheap money—especially before an election! If only the government could find a way to tie its own hands, a reliable way to resist temptation and let the citizens know that it had found a way to resist temptation.

But an elected politician *can't* tie his own hands. Even a great sailor like Odysseus needed his crew to tie his hands to the mast so he could listen to the Sirens. The mere fact that citizens know the government can't tie its own hands means that they will anticipate an inflation in advance. That means citizens start bidding up prices now, whether or not the government starts up the money printing press.

One way out: Have the government delegate total power over monetary policy to someone who doesn't care about creating a boom. And I mean someone who *really doesn't care about creating a boom*. Someone who cares only about low and stable inflation. That might be a Wall Street– or London–, or Hong Kong–based banker, someone who has spent his career worrying that high surprise inflation might crush the value of his bond portfolio.

Or it could be someone trained in real business cycle (RBC) theory, the Nobel-winning theory that modern boom-bust cycles are mostly caused by oil price changes, regulatory and tax changes, and other supply-side forces that have nothing to do with central banks and money. In its most extreme form, RBC theory means that monetary policy is irrelevant to the real economy.

But even in its milder forms, RBC theory suggests that monetary policy is overrated, that fretting about whether cheap money boosts the economy is like fretting over the decor in a hospital operating room or the color of the president's tie when he's speaking to Congress. It doesn't hurt to get it right, but only a fool spends much time worrying about it.

The moral of the story is that it's wise to delegate power over monetary policy to a conservative central banker, the more cold-hearted the better. Don't pick someone a lot like the typical citizen. Don't push for representation, for a central banker who has the same attitudes and beliefs and feelings as the typical citizen. Instead, pick someone atypical, someone who cares *less than average* about creating an economic boom: that's the way to make the average person better off. Yes, representation matters, and as Rogoff shows, representation can hurt.

Delegating Absolute Power to the Economists

So one way to make sure your government focuses on low and stable inflation is to give the job of running the central bank to someone who thinks the central bank has zero practical effect on anything *except* for inflation. Hand over the central bank to a true believer in RBC theory, a theory shaped in the early 1980s in a paper by Nobel laureates Finn Kydland and Ed Prescott, as well as a nearly simultaneous paper by University of Rochester's John Long and eventual Federal Reserve Bank president Charles Plosser. If you do that, you'll be sure the central banker will focus on the only power he thinks he has: the power to control inflation.[11]

It seems like a crazy idea, except for the fact that many of the world's leading central banks have done just that, at least to a substantial degree. The most technical economics departments have tended to do important research related to RBC theory, and central banks are likely to hire people with strong technical skills, so new PhDs trained in RBC methods are everywhere in monetary policy circles. RBC theory doesn't prove that money doesn't matter, but it gives economists another set of explanations, alternative hypotheses, to explain why the economy grows faster some years than others.

This seems to matter in real life. I mentioned that one past Federal Reserve Bank president coauthored a key RBC paper—indeed, the very paper that coined the name "real business cycles." This skepticism about the power of the central bank and the all-powerful role of economic demand shows up throughout the central banking world. I've known a few economists who have worked at central banks, and one of my favorite questions to ask them goes like this: Why do booms and busts happen? Why is economic growth volatile from year to year? The usual answer—really, the only answer I ever recall hearing—is something like, "I have no idea." I probe a bit, I get some more information, and it really does seem that people who work at central banks are fairly agnostic about whether their bosses are really doing much of anything to the real economy.

So governments may not exactly be delegating power to Rogoff's conservative central banker who cares only about inflation, and they're not exactly hiring economists who believe economic demand is irrelevant to the unemployment rate. But they've gone fairly far down that road. Central banks are often staffed and sometimes governed by economists who doubt their own power to massively change the real economy. That's one way to get central bankers to focus on the one superpower they know they have: to keep inflation low and stable.

It's the Ender's Game theory of optimal central banking. In the science-fiction novel, *Ender's Game*, a young boy, Ender Wiggin, excellent at video games, was told he was just playing a video simulation where he pretended to lead a human fleet against an alien army.[12] After his simulated fleet beat the simulated alien army, he was told that he was actually leading a real human fleet all along, acting as the de facto admiral of the human race's last-chance battle against the murderous aliens. By believing he was just playing a game, the thinking went, Ender was better able to win a real-world battle. And perhaps by thinking that they're overwhelmingly focusing on inflation, maybe independent central bankers are winning the battle for a more stable real economy.

Another way to think about Rogoff's conservative central banker theory is that it's a lot like one line of common parenting advice: in the real world, it's often best to hand over discipline to the parent who is good at saying no. That makes life easier for everyone, including the child. And technically trained economists are good at saying no to voter demands for cheaper money.

Did They Miss the Forest?

So independent central banks are more likely to fight inflation, and part of the reason is probably because they delegate power to my team: the economists. But would it be asking too much of independent central banks to also cut the risk of a massive financial crisis? Apparently not. Countries with more independent central banks appear to have fewer financial crises, not more of them. Economists Jeroen Klomp of the University of Groningen and Jakob de Haan of Munich's prestigious CESifo published a well-timed paper on the topic in 2009 just as the global financial crisis reached its peak.[13] Looking at data from a global sample weighted toward middle- and upper-middle-income countries (where more of the financial crises happen), they looked at what happened between 1980 and 2005. They measured financial distress by examining a number of dismal symptoms: falling bank credit, falling bank share values, spikes in relevant interest rates, plus many other measures.

And they didn't just check to see if there was a negative relationship between CBI and the probability of a financial crisis—Spoilers: Yes!—they went further and kicked the tires by checking to see if greater CBI predicted a lower probability of financial crisis even if you knew a lot of other things about the bank. Even if you knew the nation's level of law and order, even if you knew the nation was open to massive international financial flows, even if you knew whether the country had been hit with big shocks to the prices of its imports and exports—even then, the crude, preexisting measures of central bank independence helped predict a lower chance of a financial crisis. The link was stronger in poorer countries, but it was there in the richer ones as well.

And when Klomp and de Haan dug deeper, they found that it was the political independence of the central bank that was the real superpower. Job security for central bankers seems to make central bankers focus on their job, and part of their job is reducing the risk of a financial crisis. Maybe they do that mostly by focusing on low and stable inflation, maybe by keeping an eye on other important parts of their job like bank oversight. To dive into the details would take us too far afield. But if there's something to the complaint that independent central bankers have failed to foresee and prevent financial crises, it's worth remembering that at least from 1980 to 2005, the nonindependent central bankers usually did even worse.

Taken together, it looks like independent central banks aren't just a free lunch; they're a lunch you get paid to eat. You get low inflation, no worse (and *maybe* slightly better) growth, and a lower risk of an imploding banking system.

The Deep Roots of Independence and the Possibility of Choice

Independent central banks rarely spring out of the earth fully formed; instead, as I've hinted, they're some product of the choices of citizens, political leaders, the international investment community, and endless other factors. This brings us to a question that I've touched on but to which we now return because it's so crucial for any claims that government rules really matter. Even if less democratic central banks predict better outcomes, how can we be sure that correlation comes from, say, the long terms of the central bank governors and not from, say, the broader political culture that tolerates leaving banking to the bankers, decade in and decade out? We saw earlier that when governments increase their level of central bank independence, fairly prompt declines in inflation result, but maybe the change in CBI is just a reflection of a rapid change in the political culture. Maybe culture runs the show and political rules merely reflect culture. Is that most of the story?

Part of the answer is that of course the broader political culture shapes the setup of the central bank, the court system, and the rest of the bureaucracy. Let's look at what some economists have said after looking at long-run, cross-country data. Alberto Alesina, coauthor of the 1993 paper that made central bank independence an obsession of the field, coauthored a paper in 2010 that looked back at decades of debates on the topic. He and coauthor Andrea Stella sum up one important critique that provides "some evidence against a negative correlation of Central Bank Independence with inflation; [the authors of the critique compare] average inflation rates [against multiple] country characteristics, concluding that economic fundamentals like openness, political stability, optimal tax considerations have a much stronger impact on inflation than institutional arrangements, like central bank independence."[14]

So although Cukierman had found that CBI still helped predict lower inflation when you knew about some additional national characteristics, other researchers found that if you included other national characteristics—and I'd draw attention to the political stability measure myself—CBI became essentially useless as a predictor of lower average inflation. Princeton's Alan Blinder, after serving as the vice chairman of the Board of Governors for the U.S. Federal Reserve System, wrote in his excellent, short, blunt, not-too-technical book *Central Banking in Theory and Practice* that

> a common, but not universal, finding is that countries with more independent central banks have enjoyed lower average inflation rates without suffering lower average growth rates. . . . However at least two qualifications need to be entered. First, the notably negative correlation between central bank independence and inflation . . . is not very robust. For example, it does not hold up . . . when other variables are considered. . . . Second, some recent studies have questioned whether correlation implies causation.[15]

Despite the muddled empirical evidence, Blinder, who has been a central banker himself and has met many more central bankers the world over, still takes it as pretty obvious that central banks should be insulated, at least to some degree, from the political process. That said, he is no full-throated critic of democracy. Much of his essay is a discussion of the importance of being accountable to the citizenry, and he doesn't see democratic politicians as uniquely shortsighted. Blinder quips, "Politicians in democratic—and even undemocratic— countries are not known for either patience or long time horizons. Neither is the mass media nor the public."[16] He goes on:

> Knowing this, many governments wisely try to depoliticize monetary policy by, e.g., putting it in the hands of unelected technocrats with long terms of office and insulation from the hurly-burly of politics. . . . I conclude that central bank independence is a fine institution that ought to be preserved where it exists and emulated where it does not.[17]

Blinder knows that CBI isn't a uniquely powerful predictor of low, stable inflation, and yet he still believes that CBI is a good thing. As we've seen, there are good grounds for supporting central banks that are largely detached from day-to-day politics. We have the crude cross-country relationships in Figures 3.1, 3.2, and 3.3; we have the case studies and formal statistical analyses of countries like New Zealand that created a more independent central bank and then quickly lowered their inflation rates; and we have a good-sounding story—the parable of Rogoff's conservative central banker—that shows us how a little political detachment, in the form of some credible delegation, can go a long way toward better policy decisions.

This brings us to the question of what it means to argue for institutional reform, what it means to try to change one part of the political system when we know that the political system we live in is already shaped by voters, culture, and private economic interests at home and abroad. Why bother telling a train conductor how to steer a one-track train?

The broader question of how to give advice to people who are already hemmed in by reality is too big to ignore. In 1960, the late Harvard economist James Duesenberry made a related point, while critiquing the rational choice theory of then-future economics Nobel laureate Gary Becker: "Economics is all about how people make choices. Sociology is all about why they don't have any choices to make."[18]

I'm glad to admit that in this case, the sociologists are mostly right. But I'll still argue for small, and even for moderate-sized, political reforms, because every democratic political system seems to contain what my George Mason colleague Bryan Caplan calls *slack*—some range of political motion where a smart person with a good idea can push for a policy reform that makes things a little better.[19]

While this isn't the place to argue for the existence of free will, it is the place to argue for the existence of slack, of political wiggle room. Political choices are made from menus, and if your idea isn't on the menu, there's no chance it will be chosen. That's why this book has a lot of different ideas. Some will fit onto one nation's menu, others onto another's. And that's part of the reason why this book mostly focuses on small to medium-sized reforms. These are the reforms that a smart adviser or a small political movement can hope to slide into a bill at the last minute, reforms that often don't require a massive change in the national culture, or reforms that can conceivably be enacted in a time when voters have a fairly generic demand for change. It's usually just a bit of tinkering, even if that tinkering pushes political power 10% further away from the voters.

About That Phone Call

Years ago I heard a joke at a luncheon held in honor of Robert Mundell, the Canadian economist who had just won the Nobel. I can't recall who told the story, which went something like this:

An economics professor got a call from his old graduate school classmate. His old classmate had been born abroad, and after graduate school had returned to his home country. Now, decades later, the classmate had been appointed to run his nation's central bank. The new central bank president invites the economics professor out for a visit. The professor enters his old classmate's fine new office in the central bank headquarters, congratulates his old friend, and both take their seats and start to chat.

Soon, the banker's smartphone rings; the central banker glances at his phone and says that this is a call he has to take. Like in an old Bob Newhart bit, the professor only hears one side of the conversation:

"No."

"No."

"No."

"No."

"No."

"No."

"Yes."

"No."

"No."

"No."

And then the central banker hangs up. The puzzled professor asks his friend who that was. His old friend tells him, "That was the finance minister." Then the professor asks the obvious question: "Why did you answer 'yes' that one time?" The central banker: "He asked if I could hear him."

The room loved the joke, because it made the point that if you want to be a good central banker, you have to be Doctor No. You have to take a stand and be strong in the face of political pressure to lend to either the government or to the friends of the government. It was a simple story that explains some big facts about the political system, and it gives my fellow economists advice on how to make the system better, one No at a time.

I started this chapter with a cliché, and I'll end it with another: the best things in life are free. An independent central bank, free from the daily influence of elected politicians, free from the daily influence of democracy, is one of those best things. I noted that former Federal Reserve official Alan Blinder saw the benefits of independent central banks, but I didn't mention this passing comment he made: "While many democratic societies have independent central banks, every one leaves tax policy in the hands of elected politicians. In fact, no one even talks about turning over tax policy to an independent agency. Why? I leave this question as food for thought, perhaps for another day."[20]

In the next chapter, that day arrives.

4 The 2% Solution

Nonaccountability [e.g., restricting the power of voters to punish government officials] is most desirable when (a) the electorate is poorly informed about the optimal action, (b) acquiring decision-relevant information is costly, and (c) feedback about the quality of decisions is slow. Therefore, technical decisions, in particular, may be best allocated to judges or appointed bureaucrats.

ERIC MASKIN AND JEAN TIROLE

PRINCETON'S ALAN BLINDER HAD a whirlwind career in Washington: President Clinton asked him to serve on his Council of Economic Advisers, and then eighteen months later, Blinder took the second most powerful job at the Federal Reserve: vice chair. Nineteen months after that, he was back at Princeton. Three fast years near the pinnacles of power, and Blinder has been remarkably candid about what he learned over those three years. In an excellent essay in *Foreign Affairs*, "Is Government Too Political?" Blinder explains the differences between decision making in the White House compared to the Federal Reserve:

Regardless of who is president, life at the White House is fast paced, exhilarating, and of necessity highly political. . . . At the Federal Reserve, on the other hand, the pace is deliberate, sometimes plodding. Policy discussions are serious, even somber, and disagreements are almost always over a policy's economic, social, or legal merits, not its political marketability. . . . The Fed does not always make the right call, but its criteria are clearly apolitical. And its decisions are arguably better, on average, than those made in the political cauldron.[1]

Blinder then asks and begins to answer the big question:

What accounts for the different styles of decision-making? The White House and Congress are supposed to be political venues. Where else should a great democracy hash out its political differences? But the Fed is an independent agency. Independent of what? Well, mostly of politics.[2]

So the central bank usually makes better decisions than the politicians, and the big difference is that the central bank is independent of . . . Blinder calls it politics, but let's call it . . . democracy. Could the rest of government—or at least some of the rest—make better decisions if more power were moved away from the politicians and voters and toward independent agencies like the Fed, agencies where top appointees have long terms and are allowed to focus on policy rather than politics? I'll turn to Blinder's answer toward the end of this chapter, but first let's remember that the rich democracies already have an entire branch of government that works just like the Federal Reserve: the judiciary.

Central banks may be a part of government that's mostly run by unelected economists with long terms of office, but that's a fairly recent development. For centuries in many of the rich democracies, the judicial branch has been even more completely handed over to unelected lawyers who have long, often lifelong, terms of office. This undemocratic practice is mostly taken for granted, rarely criticized to any substantial degree. Writing about the U.S. high court in 2018, Ezra Klein of *Vox* notes, "The Supreme Court has always been undemocratic."[3]

Indeed, across the political spectrum, people applaud the undemocratic imposition of policies such as marriage equality, gun owners' rights, racially integrated schools, or radical religious liberty on an often-hostile citizenry. The "independent" judiciary—again, that code word that really means "undemocratic"—is one of the crowning achievements of the world's legal systems.

In the rich democracies, the higher courts—courts that set broad decision-making rules for trial courts—have appointees with long terms, and they make decisions by committee. For example, the European Court of Justice has twenty-eight members with six-year renewable terms (though it frequently employs smaller panels of judges), the Japanese Supreme Court has fifteen members with life tenure until age seventy, and the U.S. Supreme Court has nine members with lifetime tenure. The multimember panels dilute the power of any one judge and allow court decisions to take some advantage of the law of averages so that one mistaken judge is less likely to be the decisive vote. As a group, these judges have final, independent authority over broad swathes of legal decision making. The merits of an undemocratic judiciary are rarely questioned, and when the merits *are* questioned, the arguments rarely go beyond anecdotes and partisan complaints. But since I want to apply the logic of less democratic central banks and quite undemocratic judges to much of the rest of government—to electricity and telecommunications regulation, to city treasurers and beyond—we'll need to go beyond punditry and into the realm of scientific inquiry.

Fortunately, economists and other social scientists have collected and analyzed data to help answer the question of whether an independent judiciary is better than a political judiciary. We've just reviewed the research on central bank independence, which offers the best evidence I know of on the question of whether we're on the wrong side of the democracy-versus-bureaucracy Laffer curve. But the next largest body of statistical evidence comes from research on the judiciary. The United States in particular, with its fifty states and a variety of methods of choosing judges—partisan elections, nonpartisan elections, and nomination by expert committee are the big three—comes close to a laboratory for evaluating different ways of picking these local autocrats. And while the media often discuss morally laden judicial issues like the death penalty, abortion, and broad human rights issues, issues where the right decision is largely a matter of personal preference, judges also make quantifiable financial decisions where there's a better chance of reaching broad agreement on the best possible outcome.

All Judicial Decisions Are Local

If there's one thing you'd expect an elected judge to do, it would be to stick up for the people who put her or him into office. Amateur cynics think that means that elected judges will favor the big businesses that paid for their election campaign, but a professional cynic like me thinks that means that an elected judge will stick up for the voters. Let's look at the evidence that elected judges pay attention to the voters.

The temptation of elected judges to favor local citizens over outsiders shows up in this blunt quote from an elected judge, Richard Neely of the West Virginia Supreme Court of Appeals, the highest court in West Virginia: "As long as I am allowed to redistribute wealth from out-of-state companies to injured in-state plaintiffs, I shall continue to do so. Not only is my sleep enhanced when I give someone else's money away, but so is my job security, because the in-state plaintiffs, their families, and their friends will reelect me."[4]

Economists Eric Helland of Claremont McKenna and my George Mason colleague Alex Tabarrok found formal evidence that Neely wasn't the only judge thinking that way. Across the United States, elected judges typically favor home-state citizens. Drawing on thousands of state court lawsuit trials—torts—from 1990 to 1995, they first found evidence for the fairly obvious fact that state judges give bigger awards when the defendant—the person being sued—was from out of state rather than in state.[5] That could reflect a general bias against outsiders; it could also reflect the fact that in most states, the deepest pockets, the biggest corporations with plenty of money to pay out, are typically out of state. It's likely a bit of both, but that anti-outsider tendency isn't what's of interest here. What we care about is whether the elected judges within a given state are more generous than the appointed judges in that same state when the person being sued is out of state. And indeed elected judges *are* more generous: the average award paid by an out-of-state defendant was about $140,000 higher when the judge was elected rather than appointed.

That $140,000 difference wasn't mostly because the judges were tougher on the median losing defendant, the typical *person* who had to pay out; it's mostly because elected judges were more likely to hand out huge awards to a minority of the cases. This difference between the average (the mean) and median (the typical outcome) is worth thinking about. If you look at average (mean) awards, then a single million-dollar payout counts for more in the statistics than dozens of thousand-dollar payouts. As the cliché goes, if Mark Zuckerberg walks into my classroom, then the average person in my classroom is a billionaire—but the median person is still a thousandaire. That mean-median distinction could have been shaping the Helland-Tabarrok results, so they wisely checked to see if that was the case, and as so often when you look under the hood of a statistical analysis, that's when the results got really interesting.

First, they report that judges who get their jobs in nonpartisan elections behave about like appointed judges in their sample, so after their first tests, they pool together the appointed and nonpartisan elected judges and call the whole group "nonpartisan." The judges who run in partisan elections are the real object of interest here; they're the ones doing most of the work of getting out-of-state defendants to pay more—they're the ones acting like, well, like politicians.

If you ranked the payouts by size, the median out-of-state payout was $38,000 bigger if the judge was partisan, but the out-of-state payout at the 75th percentile—so a quarter of payouts are still bigger than that—was an amazing $304,000 larger with a partisan rather than a nonpartisan judge.

So when the payouts are well above average, partisan judges are vastly tougher than nonpartisan judges on outsiders. Is that a bad thing? Could a reasonable person make the argument that this is all for the best—that getting outsiders to pay up big time in lawsuits is better? If we see the judge's job as sticking up for the best interests of the state, perhaps getting outsiders to pay money to state citizens is a reasonable way to go about that. Or perhaps such highly visible judgments will scare away businesses that were thinking of relocating in your state—businesses surely worry about lawsuit liability when deciding where to locate. Maybe extracting more wealth from outsiders is good for the state; maybe it's bad.

I could spend the rest of this chapter trying to chase down data on both possibilities, but I won't. For us, the big message of Helland-Tabarrok is that elections matter and partisan politics matter. How we choose our judges matters for cash-on-the-table outcomes. You might think that judges are all the same—that they all went to fancy law schools, and they all socialize together, and they're all out of touch with regular folks, so it doesn't matter how they got their job. But it matters. Judges who are more independent of the voters make different decisions.

Elected Judges Are More Likely to Be Ignored by Their Colleagues

Lawyers have one favorite way to judge who's a good judge: citations. If a lot of judges refer approvingly to an old case judgment that you wrote, then you're a good judge. The law tends to be conservative in the sense that a judge likes to be able to show that her judgment is rooted in precedent, in established, well-argued principles. In real life there may be a trade-off between an "established" principle and a "well-argued" principle, since some established principles of law can be based on horrible but politically popular reasoning. But for our purposes, what matters is that when a judge is casting about for a way to come to a decision that will stick, a judgment that's less likely to be overturned by a higher court, she'll look for well-written judgments written by others in her profession.

And the legal opinion she's citing doesn't even have to be a winning judgment. Judicial dissents that you agree with are a great way to build a case for your own currently controversial view, a great way to lay the groundwork for judicial innovation. So whether you're going along with the dominant paradigm or trying to subvert it, citing old judicial precedents is a path to success.

Whose judicial opinions are more likely to be cited? In the language of the field, which judgments are "higher quality"? Opinions written by appointed judges. This question has been investigated quite a few times by different scholars, and they reach the same conclusion, so let me turn to the most comprehensive study of the issue, by Elliott Ash and W. Bentley McLeod: "Judges selected by non-partisan elections write higher-quality opinions than judges selected by partisan elections. Judges selected by technocratic merit commissions write higher-quality opinions than either partisan-elected judges or non-partisan-elected judges."[6]

The Merits of Merit Commissions

These "technocratic merit commissions" are the most common method for appointing judges in the United States, and similar methods are used the world over, so it's worth looking at what goes into them. Here's a standard case: A committee of lawyers, laypersons, and current and perhaps former judges comes up with a list of potential judicial appointees, and (in the case of U.S. states) the state's governor then picks judges from that list. Once the governor picks you, you've got the job: there's often no state senate confirmation, and never an election campaign. You just start listening to cases.

The merit commission approach varies around the world. In some countries, including India, the judges are essentially an independent, self-appointing class: judges have almost sole discretion to appoint new judges. In Israel, judges are appointed by a nine-person committee that includes three Supreme Court judges, two more lawyers who represent the Israel Bar Association, and four politicians. In practice, the lawyers defer to the judges, so the Supreme Court has broad power to choose new judges throughout the legal system, and judges have permanent appointments until age seventy. In Japan's system, judges largely appoint other judges (except for the Supreme Court, where the cabinet nominates and the emperor concurs). A Japanese

> judicial career begins with entry to the [court-run Legal Training and Research Institute] LTRI. . . . Upon graduation [from the LTRI] those interested in a judicial career apply to the Supreme Court for appointment as assistant judges. Although appointment is formally made by the cabinet from a list of nominees presented by the Supreme Court, *selection is actually made by the central personnel bureau of the Court's secretariat, which prepares the list* [emphasis added]. Assistant judges are appointed to ten-year terms. At the end of those ten years, they are eligible for appointment as full judges, again for another ten-year term. Reappointment is routine.[7]

The United Kingdom's post-2006 system of selecting judges is simple and quite independent of the voters: "Since April 2006, judicial appointments have been the responsibility of an independent Judicial Appointments Commission. . . . All appointments are made by open competition. The Commission recommends candidates to the Lord Chancellor, who has very limited power of veto."[8]

If you're interested in becoming a judge in the United Kingdom, a crucial and powerful government official, I suggest checking the jobs list at *www.judicialappointments.gov.uk*. (As of this writing, there's currently a circuit judge job available paying 135,000 pounds per year, and a spot on a high court will be available soon.) So in many countries, the extremely important judiciary is quite separate from the entire democratic process, operating on nearly a parallel path from the citizenry.

This raises the question, Why restrict this approach to judges? Countries should also consider letting committees of economic experts appoint or at least formally nominate new central bank chiefs.

A version of this process already happens quietly to some degree, since politicians sometimes discreetly ask the nation's current central banker or a few leading economists and policymakers who would make a good replacement for a retiring central bank chief. Given the apparent benefits of merit commissions for judges and since politicians are already making such inquiries quietly and informally when filling a variety of top government positions, there's good reason to encourage merit commissions for other nomination procedures. More nations should consider merit commission appointments to top jobs in independent agencies.

A relevant analogy is the executive recruitment firm. There's already a large, well-developed market in firms that help corporations pick new executives, and in my own field, a number of firms help universities search out top candidates for university presidents. In academia as in the corporate world, the process of picking a new leader works much like some state-level merit commissions: the search firm picks a few top candidates, those candidates come out for a few rounds of interviews, and then the board makes the final decision. Executive search firms rely on repeat business and reputation, so it's relatively easy to tell which executive search firms are relatively good at picking winners. Asking an executive search firm to branch out and try picking some candidates who might become a new central banker, a new supreme court justice, or a new electricity regulator wouldn't be much of a stretch. It's worth a thought.

Let's extend that thought. An executive recruitment firm would rarely restrict its search solely to people who live in the same country where the business is located. But why do national governments typically insist on hiring their own citizens? There's obviously a strong case for hiring the best talent in the world, and particularly in small countries, the best talent in the world probably lives in another country. In 2012, the British government wisely decided to hire a foreigner to run its central bank when it hired Canadian Mark Carney. Only years later did Carney eventually acquire British citizenship. Both Hong Kong and Botswana have foreign judges serving on a regular basis. And the U.S. Federal Reserve allows economists with foreign citizenship to serve in many top staff positions. Once the key political question turns from, "How do we grant maximum power to the sovereign people?" to, "How do we get the best results for the people?" the case for a government that hires the best in the world becomes far stronger. A merit commission should, barring good evidence to the contrary, search from the global talent pool. The title of President Jimmy Carter's 1975 autobiography gets it right: *Why Not The Best?*

Of course, there's no reason to think that merit commissions will be run by perfectly objective, honorable, disinterested people who care only about the public's well-being. We want them to search for the best, but any real-world merit commission will surely have its flaws and biases and its members will probably nominate a lot of their friends from college. The claim isn't that merit commissions are utopian—just that they're better than the other real-world alternatives.

The Quality of the Elected Judge

We've seen that opinions written by merit-appointed judges tend to get cited a lot. But maybe that's just because the states that have merit appointment just have better people to draw from, or maybe the judicial culture in merit-appointment states produces judges who like to cite each other a lot. What would be nice would be to look within the same state and compare some judges who were merit appointed to others who were elected. Fortunately, enough states have changed their judicial selection methods over time that we can do just that. Indeed, sometimes judges selected under different methods are sitting on the same judicial panel, writing on the very same case.

Ash and McLeod again: "We [compare] the performance of judges on the same court, making decisions in the same year, but selected under different systems."[10] Their overall conclusion, after running a variety of statistical checks: "We . . . find that compared to judges selected by voters, there is consistent evidence that judges selected by a merit commission are better at their jobs."[11]

Since merit commissions are the most common method of judicial appointment across the rich countries, it's fair to say that in practice, appointed judges are better than democratically selected judges.

An Economist's Take on Less Democratic Judges Around the World

Around the year 2000, a team of economists—Dartmouth's Rafael La Porta, Yale's Florencio Lopez-de-Silanes, Columbia's Cristian Pop-Eleches, and Harvard's Andrei Shleifer—took a serious look at the value of "judicial independence" as they called it.[12] Treating the nations of the world as separate laboratories, they checked to see if countries with judicial systems that were more independent from the political system had more of what they called "economic freedom," which they defined as "security of property rights, the lightness of government regulation, and the modesty of state ownership."

A voluminous empirical literature in economics shows that measures of economic freedom tend to be reasonably good predictors of current prosperity and future economic progress, and they capture Adam Smith's theoretical prediction that a high degree of economic laissez-faire tends to make a nation more productive and the typical citizen more prosperous. Since economic theory and evidence tell largely the same story, one wonders whether judicial independence helps create at least a bit more laissez-faire. And after spending the last few pages looking mostly at the U.S. experience, it's time to return to a global outlook.

Their measure of judicial independence combines three features:

- The term length of supreme court judges

- The term length of administrative court judges (often in charge of enforcing regulations created by the nation's top executive, not by the legislature)

- Whether judges pay explicit attention to the decisions of past judges—that is, whether case law is a key ingredient in each judge's decision-making recipe

Note that the first two have some overlap with measures of central bank independence (long terms mean you're less accountable to the person who hired you), and the third has some overlap with our earlier measure of what makes for a good judge (sticking fairly close to old decisions creates predictability in the society).

At the raw level of correlation, La Porta and his colleagues find these good outcomes in countries with more judicial independence. First, private property rights have stronger protection (so it's harder for the government to just take your house without paying you for it, for instance). Second, it takes fewer steps to legally start a new business (less red tape). Third, there tend to be fewer employment regulations (so hiring is less like an undivorceable marriage). And finally, the government owns less of the banking system. Note that government-owned banks are key mechanisms that politicians use to steer funds to their favored groups, even though government-owned banks typically tend to hurt the economy as a whole.

All of these raw correlations tend to be moderate to strong relationships. So at the most basic level, greater judicial independence predicts (even if it may not cause) a lot of traits associated with national prosperity.

The next question is whether this correlation reflects much cause and effect. Maybe countries get rich because of a high savings rate or having good weather, and *then* they go out and buy fancy luxury goods like air-conditioning, low corruption, and judicial independence. That's a possibility, so the authors do what social scientists almost always do: check to see if a nation's level of judicial independence can still help you predict the four good outcomes I listed even if you already know things like the country's income per person (maybe judicial independence is just a luxury good, not a cause of pro-market policy outcomes), how far the nation is from the equator (since nations close to the equator tend to be less productive), or the nation's level of ethnic and linguistic diversity (since diversity is a frequent predictor of political conflict that might hurt the economy, hurt the political system, and make judicial independence difficult).

In some bonus results, the authors also check to see if perhaps the real reason judicial independence predicts pro-market policy outcomes is that countries with independent judiciaries are also extremely likely to have British common law legal systems. Maybe the common law system—with not just a respect for judicial precedent, but usually accompanied by the full quiver of respect for property rights, rights of judicial appeal, jury trials, and all the rest—is the central driver of these raw correlations. Maybe we don't need independent judiciaries with long terms; maybe we just need to hand out copies of Blackstone's legendary *Commentaries on the Laws of England.*

So they checked that too. And in the end, it turns out that their simple three-variable index of judicial independence still does a very good job of predicting stronger private property rights. Maybe the conventional wisdom is right and judges who hold their jobs for a long time and pay attention to past decisions are more willing to say "No!" when government officials want to take somebody's house to build a highway or tell a business owner she can't sell her engineering firm to a politically unpopular conglomerate.

It turns out that even if you know that a nation officially uses British common law, even if you know how rich it is, how far from the equator, and how much diversity it has, greater judicial independence is still a robust predictor of stronger private property rights. By my reading of the paper by La Porta and his colleagues, greater judicial independence is also a solid predictor of less government ownership of banks, less labor market regulation, and less red tape to start a new business. (That's a personal interpretation. Interpreting statistical results sometimes is a bit like evaluating a painting, a matter of taste.)

Here's how the authors themselves sum up their original, raw correlation results:

> Reducing judicial independence from . . . the United States [level]
> to . . . [the] Vietnam [level does the following]

[It] reduces the property rights index . . . roughly [from the U.S. level] to Mexico or Nepal and halfway toward Vietnam,

[It] raises the number of procedures on new entry . . . roughly to Italy or South Korea and two-thirds of the way toward Vietnam . . .

[It] raises employment regulation . . . roughly to Belgium or Turkey and almost all the way to Vietnam . . .

[It] raises government ownership of banks by 42 percentage points (roughly to Norway or Ecuador and compared to 99 percent for Vietnam).[13]

Making all of the fancy statistical adjustments I've mentioned cuts these relationships in half at most, and it cuts the property rights relationship back by only a third. If you're trying to guess how laissez-faire an economy is, you could do a lot worse than to ask whether that nation's top judges have terms of fewer than six years. And there's good reason to believe that a lot of that is cause and effect. Elected politicians don't want to spend too much time fighting independent judges, and independent judges, like central bankers, are more likely than politicians to focus on the long run, on the big picture.

Post-Judicial Interlude

Perhaps the time you've spent reading the first half of the chapter was time wasted. Most people in the rich, relatively low-corruption democracies take the undemocratic judiciary for granted. They see it as naturally a strength of "democracy" that our judges aren't . . . what's the word? Oh yes: "political." But for me, it was important to think about just why undemocratic judges are a great idea— the long time horizons; the productive, heavily recycled form of decision making we call "judicial precedent"; the apparent effects on economic freedom—because those reasons for having undemocratic judges are probably going to turn out to be good reasons to make other government agencies and other government offices at least a little less democratic.

Take It from Me: Don't Let People Vote for the Local Treasurer

> Holding officials directly accountable to voters can result in lower
> levels of performance in complex policy areas.
>
> Alexander Whalley

Economist Alexander Whalley of the University of Calgary looked at an elected job that combines a need for trustworthy behavior with a need for mastery of financial detail: city treasurer. Treasurers have the boring, technical, yet important responsibilities of making sure the city's money isn't stolen or lost, that taxes are paid on time, and that the city pays its own bills on time. On top of all this, treasurers handle the borrowing. They might ask small commercial banks for short-term credit lines to pay firefighters before the year's property taxes come in, or they might go to large investment banks to help arrange a bond sale to borrow millions or even hundreds of millions of dollars for a decade.

These are all tasks where corruption and incompetence are real possibilities, and where that same corruption and incompetence will make banks and investors reluctant to lend to the city. I come from Orange County, California, which in 1994 became what was at the time "the largest municipality in U.S. history to declare bankruptcy."[14] So I've thought a little about the question of whether treasurers should be elected or appointed. But before I tell you the Orange County story, let's see what Whalley found.

Some cities in California appoint their treasurers and others elect their treasurers. Cities can have elections to decide whether the city treasurer should be appointed by the city government; the default is that they're elected. Whalley checks to see which kinds of cities have lower borrowing costs: ones with appointed treasurers or elected ones. The interest rate paid on a city's debt is a useful index of how well the city is running its finances. Managing a city's borrowing costs is complicated. Making your case to the financial system that your city is a good credit risk means focusing on a lot of details, and there are a lot of financial institutions that would love to make a California city pay high interest costs. If you can bring your city's borrowing costs down by just a few tenths of a percent each year, you're doing a great job. So Whalley's overall question is this: Do cities with appointed treasurers pay lower interest rates on their debt?

Any particular California city might have lots of reasons for paying a different interest rate from the city next door. It might have a lot of citizens with lower education levels, it might have a lot of children enrolled in school who eat up revenue and whose parents aren't paying much in taxes, or it might just be a small city that could be put at risk if one big employer moves out of town. A more obvious reason might just be that one city might start off with a lot more debt than another. Whalley shows that even if you know all of those facts about a California city, plus many more, the appointed treasurers are able to get lower interest rates on the city debt—about half a percentage point lower on average— than elected officials. In his basic tests, appointed treasurers win hands down.

But maybe there's some other feature of the city that he didn't quite catch—a statistical *je ne sais quoi*. He has two more tricks up his sleeve from the standard statistical tool kit. First, he treats every city as its own experiment and looks just at differences in interest rates before and after a city switches to having an appointed treasurer. Over the period Whalley examined, 1992 to 2008, forty-three cities held referenda to ask whether they should switch to appointed treasurers. He's therefore able to look at the before-and-after differences of these elections in two ways, and the second is worth our attention: regression discontinuity design (RDD). That's roughly equivalent to comparing interest rates in cities that *just barely* voted for an appointed treasurer (like a 51% vote) to interest rates in cities that *just barely* rejected an appointed treasurer (like a 49% vote). In a case like that, a city that just barely accepts is probably a lot like a city that just barely rejects, so this is as close to an experiment as we're likely to get outside a petri dish.

This RDD method finds an even bigger benefit of appointed treasurers: seven-tenths of a percent lower interest rates every year. The average city in the sample has about $30 million in debt, so that comes out to a savings of $210,000 per year. It's probably worth giving up some local voice to get those savings.

The story of city treasurers offers a great argument for appointed jobs and a great way to ridicule a key argument for elections. One of the folk arguments for electing government officials is "accountability." Citizens, the story goes, need to be able to hold elected officials accountable, and one way to hold them accountable is to retain the right to fire and replace them. But in the case of city treasurers, it's easy to measure (much of) the job the treasurer is doing: just look at the interest rate on the city debt. But even when such a key quality index is so easy to measure, voting citizens do an awful job of keeping the city treasurer accountable. The better option is to let other city officials—the elected mayor, the city council, or maybe the appointed city manager—pick a treasurer and then keep an eye on the job she's doing. Those city officials will surely notice if the treasurer is saving the city over $200,000 a year, even if voters are too preoccupied watching cat videos to do the job.

This brings me to my childhood home, to Orange County, California, home to Disneyland, In-N-Out Burger, and the Nixon Presidential Library. The county itself has a separate government from the cities, and it runs quite a few programs and organizations. For instance, it's in charge of John Wayne Airport, the sheriff's office, and many public works projects. The county government is run by an elected board of supervisors, and it also has a treasurer. In the mid-1990s, when financial derivatives were first becoming a retail financial product, the county treasurer, Robert Citron, made the mistake of investing some of the county's money in these derivatives, which were really bets that the nation's interest rates would stay low. Instead, they rose—as the Federal Reserve tightened money early in the Clinton administration—and the treasurer lost a ton of the county's money. Rather than admit his error, he essentially gambled for double or nothing on his bets—and you can guess how that turned out. Even the psychic whom Citron (actually!) consulted failed to find a solution to the problems Citron created.

Within a few months, the county filed for bankruptcy. County services largely kept running, and it was mostly bond investors who took a bath. So who or what was to blame? The county sued Merrill Lynch, saying the bank gave the treasurer bad financial advice. Many regular voters in Orange County blamed the Democrats, since the county treasurer was a registered Democrat in a county that was then heavily Republican. But you can guess a major reason he did a poor job, even if it's only part of the story. It didn't start with a "D" or an "R." It probably started with an "E."

Electricity and Telecom Regulation: Top of the Laffer Curve?

Government regulators are another area where elections and appointments are two key alternatives. Partly because so many economists and lawyers are deeply involved in these industries—I'm told the consulting gigs are well paid, whether you're working for the government or for the regulated industries—there's been a lot of research on the subject. As with judges, the methods of selection vary across time and space, so we can compare a lot of before-and-afters and a lot of here-and-theres. As usual, it's not truly an experiment, but it's better than just throwing around anecdotes.

So which method is better? Is this going to be as clear-cut as the central bank independence research? Whalley himself says in a footnote: "There is large literature on the effects of appointed and elected regulators that has generally found mixed results."[15] If that turns out to be the case, then that's okay; it would suggest that there's no big difference if your nation picks elected regulators or appointed regulators, and it's a mere matter of taste. In a world where voters are routinely told that every election has earth-shaking consequences, it'd be comforting to hear that this time around, nothing much is at stake. Economists have to remind each other that that's typically what happens when you're making roughly the right choice. If you make a small mistake and buy a car that's a little too fancy or you mistakenly keep your restaurant open an hour later than usual on Thursday nights, it won't make that much of a difference. When you're close to the optimal choice, a small mistake usually means you lose some benefits, but you lose just about the same amount of costs, so together the changes come close to cancelling out.

Related: How do you check to see if you're at the top of a mountain? By looking around to see if any place nearby is higher than where you are right now. And one way to tell if you're near the top of the mountain is if almost everything around you is sky. That's the way some researchers view the elected-versus-appointed regulator literature: one option isn't obviously better than the other, so in their view, you're close to the optimum regardless of your choice. That's what it looks like when you're near the top of the democracy Laffer curve: mostly sky.

Captured Regulators: A Reason for Worry

One risk of appointed regulators is that they'll end up caving to the demands of industry insiders. Whether through explicit bribes or the promise of future jobs, industry incumbents—the big telephone companies, the big electricity companies—might be able to convince regulators to let regulated utilities rip off consumers and businesses. People need their phones and need their electricity, and there's a lot of monopoly power there to exploit, so regulated businesses have a strong incentive to pressure any regulator for higher prices and lax quality requirements.

The theory of regulator capture has some overlap with President Dwight Eisenhower's worries about the military-industrial complex, which Ike discussed in a shocking and powerful speech toward the end of his presidency. He wanted to tell Americans that they needed to be vigilant about monitoring both the military and military contractors. He warned that in the post–World War II era, this conjunction of an immense military establishment and a large arms industry is new in the American experience. The total influence—economic, political, even spiritual—is felt in every city, every State house, every office of the Federal government. We recognize the imperative need for this development. Yet we must not fail to comprehend its grave implications. . . .

In the councils of government, we must guard against the acquisition of unwarranted influence, whether sought or unsought, by the military-industrial complex. The potential for the disastrous rise of misplaced power exists and will persist.

We must never let the weight of this combination endanger our liberties or democratic processes. We should take nothing for granted. Only an alert and knowledgeable citizenry can compel the proper meshing of the huge industrial and military machinery of defense with our peaceful methods and goals, so that security and liberty may prosper together.[16]

Note that top military officials and top electricity regulators have something in common: they're both interacting closely with the same small number of large businesses on a regular basis, and it's often the government official's job to give bad news to those large businesses. A regulator might turn down an electricity price increase, and a top general might turn down a new, deeply flawed weapons program after the military contractor has already spent tens of millions in research and development.

Judges, by contrast, even judges who focus on large civil cases, are likely to deal with a vast, ever-changing variety of industries. In fact, it's common for cases to be assigned to judges randomly. From the point of view of a private business, buying off a judge for a decade or two—through, say, the promise of a plum job after retirement—is a riskier investment than buying off a regulator or a top admiral with a similar promise. If your firm needs the judge only once or twice over two decades, then maybe the soft bribe of a future job is worth it, but probably not. But when your business is dealing with the same government officials month in and month out, it's far easier to see the winning financial case for owning a regulator—or for owning an admiral with a lot of influence over naval radar procurement.

The cynical, and thus plausible, case for electing electricity and telecom regulators is that the fear of looming elections will discourage regulators from selling out completely to the industries they regulate. The power of voters is a form of what Harvard economist John Kenneth Galbraith used to call "countervailing power": power that has a chance to stand up to dangerous forces.

But just because there's a problem doesn't mean there's an easy solution. The risks of the military-industrial complex that Ike warned about are real, but that doesn't mean we should be voting for our admirals. There are benefits and costs to democratic checks on insider power, and as we've already seen, it's pretty likely that in the case of judges, central bankers, and city treasurers, we're probably better off with the devil of insider influence than with the devil of democratic influence.

Maybe those lessons apply to regulators, or maybe not: the tale of the tape will tell. That's one reason academic researchers dive into such deep detail to see if less democratic appointed regulators are better or worse than more democratic elected regulators. Measurement matters.

Shortsighted Voters, Fearful Investors, and a Repeated Theme

The United States is the most widely studied case for electricity regulation, so it will be our starting point. Tim Besley of the London School of Economics and Stephen Coate of Cornell report the following patterns, partly based on their own work and partly based on the work of others:[17]

- In states with elected electricity regulators, consumer electricity rates are lower compared to states with appointed electricity regulators.

- In states with elected electricity regulators, public utilities have lower bond ratings and pay higher interest rates—about a quarter of a percent higher on average.

- In states with elected electricity regulators, there's noisy evidence that overall points toward more blackouts and less quality improvement after previous blackouts.

The evidence on the effects of elected electricity regulators isn't as conclusive as the evidence for the costs of voter-dependent central banks. But taken together, it's consistent with a simple freshman economics story where elected regulators tend to impose price ceilings for consumer electricity—a little like rent control—thus keeping prices low but at the cost of keeping the quantity (and quality) of supply low. The lower mandated prices are likely to cause less investment in electricity infrastructure. That means that with price ceilings, you might get more brownouts or blackouts, or it might be harder to build a new subdivision amid the restricted electricity supply, but for most consumers, the low rates feel like a free lunch.

This first take at interpreting the facts flows from the economist's instinctive revulsion toward price controls. We can tell you all about their obvious visible benefits and the hidden costs: you'll be happy about the lower costs when power is up and running, but when the power goes out, you probably won't blame years of price controls for the thirty-minute loss of power.

That's one way to explain the facts: elected electricity regulators create artificial shortages, but most voters are okay with that, partly because most don't know whom to blame when things go wrong.

There's another way to explain these facts, one with a long and noble tradition in the field of regulatory economics. Because governments often promise regulated industries a guaranteed "rate of return"—roughly a profit percentage—on every dollar's worth of equipment they invest in the industry, regulated industries like electricity have a strong incentive to get as big as regulators will allow. A 7% rate of return on $10 million in capital equipment is a lot more money than a 7% rate of return on $5 million in capital equipment. This way of looking at the same facts means there's a pretty good argument for voters as a form of "countervailing power" even if it means less electricity capacity. Appointed regulators cave to the call

THE 2% SOLUTION   85

of utility providers to become big, but elected regulators turn a more skeptical eye and tend to keep the utilities small. Since government-created energy gluts are a waste of perfectly good resources, maybe some shortsighted voters who insist on low consumer prices are a practical fix for this chronic problem of expensive oversupply.

That means that two theories can fit the same small set of facts, a fairly common outcome in any serious inquiry—it's hard for an outsider to tell exactly how big or how robust a local utility network should be, even an outsider with access to lots of data. But there's room for more thought on the topic. Dino Falaschetti, an economist at the Hoover Institution at Stanford University, looked at the telecommunications industry in the United States through the lens of freshman economics, and by paying attention to the details, he noticed something others had apparently missed: "This established theoretical setup yields a clear observable implication—i.e., if electing regulators expands [economic] surplus, then *jurisdictions that elect regulators should be associated with relatively high levels of output* [emphasis added]."[18]

Falaschetti realized that if consumers were doing a good job picking regulators, they'd choose regulators who set the price low enough so that consumers would want to buy a lot of telecom services! And at the same time, if consumers were doing a good job picking regulators, they'd choose regulators who set the price *just* high enough that telecom firms would still be willing to build out a network big enough to meet that high demand for cheap telecom services: cheap enough to be easily affordable, abundant enough to provide high-quality streams of James Brown's "Star Time" on a Saturday night. That's what a good consumer-focused regulator would get you. If consumers are going to exploit the capitalists, the consumers should at least get high-quality digital content out of the deal.

But Falaschetti shows that elected telecom regulators instead oversee regions with "significantly smaller quantities of local [telecom] exchange services than do those where commissioners are appointed."[19]

Falaschetti offers one possible explanation for why the simple optimistic theory of democratic regulation goes awry: the "capital levy problem." In many regulated industries, the up-front fixed cost of capital investment is huge compared to the day-to-day marginal cost of running the industry. Utility networks are expensive to build, but keeping them going after they're built is relatively cheap. So regulated industries fear that consumers will make up-front promises like this: "Hey, sure, we'll gladly pay a high enough electricity price to cover both your building costs and your day-to-day costs" (fixed and marginal cost, respectively, in economics jargon). But after the network is built, after the electricity plants are completed and it's more a matter of paying for this week's coal supply and this month's maintenance costs, consumers will ask themselves, "Why are we paying so much for electricity when it's so cheap to produce?"

Then, the capital levy story goes, consumers will demand that regulators cut the price of electricity down toward the marginal cost of electricity production. That means the people who paid for the factories to be built never get repaid because the price is high enough to cover day-to-day costs, but not much more. The final result is that consumers get the benefits of cheap electricity without having to pay most of the up-front costs. The consumers, in economics jargon, have extracted a capital levy.

That sounds like a sob story, but it's a sob story that no public utility CEO wants to live through, and as a result, utilities invest less in places with elected regulators in Falaschetti's story. They don't want to get left holding the bag, so they never pick up the bag in the first place. And notice that the capital levy problem has strong parallels with Rogoff's conservative central banker from Chapter 3: if you leave the voters in charge of utility regulation, you'll likely get fewer services, less reliable services, or both. The voters' willingness to alter the deal—like Darth Vader did with Lando in *Empire Strikes Back*—makes that industry reluctant to strike big deals with voters in the first place. But if you delegate utility regulation to the trained experts—maybe even to experts who are friendly with industry—you'll get a higher quantity and quality of service, at a slightly higher price.

One more fact, this time from a widely cited survey of the elected-versus-appointed regulator issue, again from Besley and Coate: "We also show that states with elected regulators are less likely to pass through cost changes into prices."[20] This isn't a clinching piece of evidence in favor of appointed regulators, but it's annoyingly memorable. If there's one big idea in economic theory, one that matters for monopolies and fiercely competitive firms alike, it's that if a firm is acting by an invisible hand for the benefit of society, then it's going to raise prices when costs go up and cut prices when costs go down. For firms to send society the right signals about what's abundant and what's scarce, prices need to reflect real-world information about scarcity. Perhaps the finest version of the message was told by the Nobel laureate Friedrich Hayek in his wondrous essay "The Use of Knowledge in Society":

> Fundamentally, in a system where the knowledge of the relevant facts is dispersed among many people, prices can act to coördinate the separate actions of different people. . . . It is worth contemplating for a moment a very simple and commonplace instance of the action of the price system to see what precisely it accomplishes. Assume that somewhere in the world a new opportunity for the use of some raw material, say, tin, has arisen, or that one of the sources of supply of tin has been eliminated. It does not matter for our purpose—and it is very significant that it does not matter—which of these two causes has made tin more scarce. All that the users of tin need to know is that some of the tin they used to consume is now more profitably employed elsewhere and that, in consequence, they must economize tin.[21]

So if tin—or coal, or oil, or windpower or waterpower—becomes scarce, markets tend to deliver the bad news. Appointed regulators are more likely to let regulated industries behave, at least in this way, more like an efficient, competitive market. They're more likely, at least in this way, to let market signals do their job. You can imagine why elected regulators are more likely to keep retail electricity prices stable when electricity costs fluctuate: if you cut prices when the good news comes along, you'll have to raise prices when the bad news comes along. And if there's one thing we know about voters—about human beings in general—it's that they obsess over bad news, which of course gets politicians thrown out of office. So from the point of view of an elected electricity regulator, it's probably better to give no news at all rather than a mix of good and bad news. As I think the saying goes, "No news is news of a clear path to reelection."

There's Independence—and Then There's Independence

In Europe and in the U.S. federal (as opposed to state) government, there's no real option for elected regulators. Instead the options on the organizational menu are closer to the case for central banks: Are the regulators easy to fire? Do they have long terms? And of course these aren't the only measures of regulator independence. In a study of European telecom regulators, the authors' index of regulator independence included features such as these:

- Whether the regulator oversaw multiple issues (like telecom plus electricity plus water), perhaps since, as with judges, it's harder to buy off a regulator who only thinks about your industry less than half the time.

- Whether the regulatory body has multiple members (a version of the law of large numbers we saw earlier; and perhaps it's harder to buy off half of a regulatory panel than it is to buy off just one regulator).

- Does the regulator have to report to two branches—the executive and the legislative—or just one? Just as a child can get away with more when she can play off one parent from another, so too can a regulator act more independently if she has two masters.[22]

This is a reminder: With central bankers as with industry regulators, independence isn't a toggle switch; it's a matter of degree. And remembering whom you have to be independent *of* is crucial. Yes, it's often the shortsighted, ill-informed voters you need to resist, but the authors of this study, London-based researchers Geoff Edwards and Leonard Waverman, found that the strongest benefit of independent regulators was that independence helped regulators say no to the government itself.

They looked at data from "the original 15 EU member states over seven years (1997–2003)" to see how independence affected a crucial element of competition: How much were big incumbent telecoms allowed to charge to upstart newcomers that wanted to interconnect through the incumbents' networks?[23] So if a new France-based telecom wants to connect a call from France to Sweden by way of Germany, is the German telecom allowed to set a discriminatory high price just for newbies, perhaps as a ploy to curtail competition? Or does the regulator insist that the German telecom set a lower price, close to cost and close to the apparent prices that it charges other established competitors? This example is, of course, an illustration (details vary from year to year, industry to industry), but the question of whether new firms will be treated—let's go ahead and use the word *fairly*—will shape whether your industry winds up with healthy competition between firms or with just a few high-priced regional monopolies.

Edwards and Waverman found a clear result. Yes, regulator independence predicted lower (fairer!) interconnect prices, but that was driven by one crucial feature: whether the regulator was confronting a government-owned telecom. Professors often worry about whether big business will distort market competition, but it turns out that the old bumper sticker has a lot going for it: "Don't steal: the government hates the competition." Independent regulators were apparently more likely to stand up against telecoms owned by big government.

Measuring true regulator independence of course involves a mix of art and science, of general rules and local knowledge. As with central bank independence, any measure of regulator independence is only a noisy measure of what we really care about—whether the regulator feels she has the power to say no. A World Bank report cautiously recommending greater regulator independence makes a relevant point here: no mere index of independence can fully capture true regulator independence: "Some argue that governance traditions in some countries make independence illusory—'If the Palace calls, the regulator will comply.' Certainly, adopting even the most sophisticated law will not magically transform the basic institutional environment. Nevertheless . . . creating such agencies is worth the effort, even in more challenging environments."[24]

The Golden Rule of Independence

In this chapter and the previous one, there's one element of independence that I haven't mentioned so far—but shows up often when lawyers discuss the question of agency independence: *Who pays the bills?* In the United States, according to Lisa Schultz Bressman and Robert Thompson, both of Vanderbilt, "several of the [finance-oriented] independent agencies have funding sources, usually from users and industry, which frees them from dependence on congressional appropriations and annual budgets developed by the executive branch."[25]

Regulatory agencies are just like Regency romance novels: to feel a certain personal independence, it's important to have a clear financial independence. The power of the purse is something that regulators respect. The most famous case of financial independence in the United States is that of the Federal Reserve, which has total discretion in how it spends the interest on the investments it holds and how it spends the money it earns from the fees it receives for clearing millions of checks every day. I've been fortunate enough to eat at various Federal Reserve banks when attending research conferences, and I can tell you that they aren't spending the money on the food and wine, or if they are, they're wildly overpaying. And in fact, the Fed returns the overwhelming majority of the fees and interest they earn each year. So whatever price we're paying to let my fellow economists run the Federal Reserve System, it's likely worth it as long as we're getting low and stable inflation.

The case for financially independent regulatory agencies is just a matter of applying to regulators the intuition that America's founders had about judges: Article III of the U.S. Constitution states, "The Judges, both of the supreme and inferior Courts, shall . . . at stated Times, receive for their Services, a Compensation, which shall not be diminished during their Continuance in Office." If Congress doesn't like a federal judge, they can't starve her out of office by cutting her pay to a dollar a year. They have to impeach and remove her, in meetings akin to a court of law. They actually do this every so often. The most recent impeachments of U.S. federal judges were in 2009 and 2010, and both involved horrible crimes. One judge resigned before he could be removed from office, and the other was both removed and barred from ever again holding federal office.

Few regulatory agencies are going to get funding guarantees written into their nation's constitution, so an independent funding stream is the next best path. For instance, in their study of European telecom regulation, Edwards and Waverman treat fee-based funding as a sign of regulatory independence: having to ask the government for annual appropriations, in their view, obviously weakens the political independence of the regulator. The independent funding streams will differ from regulator to regulator: citizens could let antitrust regulators collect and keep the fees from the industries they regulate so they can avoid asking the legislature for an extra statistician who can help crunch data. Let the nation's patent office impose a small tax on patent applications so the office doesn't have to face down the legislature's appropriations committee each year—and indeed, this is actually the case in the United States since its Patent and Trademark office pays for itself through fees.

This approach should obviously be expanded. If the legislature gets really upset about how the regulator is spending the fee revenue, it can always hold a special hearing—but otherwise let's give regulators about 10% more distance from democracy.

Appointed Legislators: The Blinder Proposal
The quote that begins this chapter—by Nobel laureates Maskin and Tirole—suggests that when it's crucial to get the technical details right and when the policy debate is less about values and

more about facts and competent execution, that's likely a good opportunity to delegate power to unelected bureaucrats. Princeton's Alan Blinder has been thinking along the same lines for over two decades. As we saw at the end of the previous chapter, after his time in the White House and at the Fed, Blinder pondered whether tax legislation would be better handled by an organization like the Federal Reserve rather than the way it's handled now: through a political battle between Congress and the president. He fleshed out these thoughts in an excellent 1997 essay in *Foreign Affairs*, entitled "Is Government Too Political?" In 2018 he returned to the same issue, this time at book length. The end product, *Advice and Dissent: Why America Suffers When Economics and Politics Collide*, retains one of the great strengths of his earlier writings about American politics: candor about the way things way things really work in DC. He starts the book off with a good story. In January 1993, President-elect Bill Clinton, a man who knows something about how politics really works, gave Blinder some sage advice on how to how to pose for a photo-op: "Alan, now you're supposed to say nothing and look profound."[26]

Alas, that's not just advice for looking good on the front page of the *New York Times*. It's often what politicians hope economists will do when asked for advice: stay quiet and give the impression that the intellectual heavyweights support whatever the politicians decide on—experts as window dressing.

Blinder hopes for more than that. Indeed, he insists that a well-run country *needs* more than that. And since he's a strong supporter of independent central banks, he suggests extending that approach to tax policy. And while he doesn't suggest a precise *percentage*, Blinder recognizes that his approach might well slightly reduce a nation's level of democracy: "What I meant to suggest twenty years ago, and even more so today, is that a few economic policy decisions might be made better by technocrats than by politicians—and with no substantial diminution of democracy."[27] Is 10% substantial? I'd say so, though just barely—so perhaps Professor

Blinder is thinking more about a 2% diminution of democracy. A good place to start.

After running through a few areas where the U.S. government already has allowed unelected experts to run most of the show— monetary policy, fast-track trade treaty authority, and the 1990s military base closings—Blinder turns to his big proposal: "[A] Federal Tax Board (FTB) patterned on the Federal Reserve Board. Its members would be presidential appointees, confirmed by the Senate for long terms."[28]

We're in familiar territory now, applying the wisdom of independent central banks to the tax code. Here's his sample FTB charter: "The board shall design, implement, and maintain a tax system that promotes the long-run growth of the economy with due respect to the goals of fairness, simplicity, and efficiency."[29] He suggests that Congress should decide the broad parameters (What fraction of national income should the federal government take in the average year? What percentage of the taxes should by paid by the top 1% of earners? What share should be paid by corporations versus individuals?) and then let the FTB do its job. Let Congress decide on the values, let the FTB iron out the details. Blinder is quite certain that such a system would be far superior to the status quo: "The FTB could go to work designing tax laws that are much fairer, far simpler, and immensely less distortionary than those we have now."[30]

He's right. If there's one thing we know about tax experts, it's that they'd never design a tax code as cumbersome as the one we have. And if there's one thing we know about legislators, it's that they can't resist the temptation to carve out one more special exception in the tax code, for either a favored corporation or an emotionally resonant, politically organized group of activists. When the cameras are off, politicians pander to the powerful; when the cameras are on, they pander to us. Either way, it means a tax code full of carve-outs—Swiss cheese, but for funding the commonweal.

Blinder's FTB would be a big step forward for delegated authority, for giving legislative power to unelected experts, and it's a policy that any rich democracy could embrace. More than that, it opens a window to a world where elected officials stick to their strength: listening to voters and setting broad parameters. For centuries, democracies have left the actual execution of the law to unelected bureaucrats, while slowly moving in the direction of leaving more and more of the details of law—the regulations and procedures that flesh out the minutiae—to those same bureaucrats. The best evidence suggests that if the rich democracies take more steps in that same direction, there's a good chance of big benefits with little risk of big costs. Those are the kinds of steps it's smart to take.

I'll close with Blinder's conclusions on the merits of handing legislative power to his FTB: "Is technocratic tax writing a wise thing to do for the public interest? . . . Some might argue no . . . that conferring so much power on a group of unelected technocrats is undemocratic. They have a point. But I disagree, for many of the same reasons that underpin the independence of the Federal Reserve."[31]

After reviewing the democratic checks included in his FTB proposal—essentially the same as the democratic checks on rich-country central banks—he concludes with words that embrace the wisdom of 2% less democracy "Such judgments are always in the eyes of the beholder, but that list creates enough political legitimacy for me."[32]

5   This Chapter Does Not Apply to Your Country

The question now is whether most adults are sufficiently
competent to participate in governing the state. Are they?

ROBERT DAHL

THE AMERICAN CONVENTION ON HUMAN RIGHTS, drafted in 1969,
signed by dozens of states across Latin America, and in force since
1978, says that the right to vote can legitimately be taken away
from those who don't have enough education. And that's not the
only legitimate path to losing the right to vote, according to the
Convention. To quote from Article 23:

> Every citizen shall enjoy the following rights and opportunities . . .
> to vote and to be elected in genuine periodic elections, which shall
> be by universal and equal suffrage and by secret ballot that guaran-
> tees the free expression of the will of the voters. . . .

> The law may regulate the exercise of the rights and opportunities
> referred to in the preceding paragraph only on the basis of age,
> nationality, residence, language, *education, civil and mental capac-
> ity, or sentencing by a competent court* [emphasis added] in criminal
> proceedings.[1]

The UN's High Commission on Human Rights is well aware of
the convention's potential restrictions on the right to vote. In one
recent book, the High Commission draws attention to one of the
above restrictions: "Article 20 [of an earlier declaration on human

rights] guarantees the right to vote and participate in government, but article 23 of the Convention permits these rights to be limited on the basis of, inter alia, language."[2]

This convention is still in force for twenty-three of the original twenty-five signatory nations, including the large, middle- to upper-middle-income nations of Mexico, Brazil, Argentina, and Chile. This portion of the treaty has never been stricken. Restrictions on the right to vote, based solely on the level of a person's education, are within the range of international law.

The core question for our purposes, of course, is not whether such restrictions are *legal* but whether they are *wise*. For instance, if a high school diploma were a prerequisite for voting, would a rule like that improve government quality? Before turning to that question, let's try another one first. If those with *more* than a high school education were forbidden from voting, what would happen to the quality of government? Think about that for a moment.

You can see where this is going. Informed voters matter in democracies, and while there are lots of exceptions, the rule is clear: the more educated tend to know more about how government works and about how different policy proposals—even well-intentioned ones—may or may not work as planned.

On average, more educated voters bring more information and more intelligence into the voting booth. Since politicians pander to voters, not to nonvoters, then any improvement in the skill level, the information level, or the human capital of voters will mean that politicians will be pandering to customers who know more about the product. A broad swath of political thought, formal and informal, philosophical and empirical, strongly suggests that voters who know more about politics and policy and the world around them are likely to push the government in a wiser direction.

Before I turn to that line of reasoning, let's ask just how restrictive a universal high school diploma voting requirement would be. We'll find out that it will often be too restrictive—and it should be opposed when it is—but let's look at the facts first. Within the rich democracies, the focus of this book, the vast majority of citizens graduate from high school, and across these countries, the majority of most of the widely studied ethnic and cultural groups also graduate from high school. For example, in Japan, over 85% of members of the historically disadvantaged Ainu ethnic group aged forty and under have completed twelve years of school.[3] One government study of English data reported that in recent years, no ethnic group analyzed in the study—including those of Caribbean African descent, Pakistani descent, and Indian descent—had less than a 70% passage rate on the General Certificate of Secondary Education battery of exams, the equivalent of a high school diploma.[4] And in the United States, among those who begin ninth grade, 91% of Asian American/Pacific Islanders, 76% of African Americans, and 79% of Hispanic-Americans graduate on time with a high school diploma four years later.[5]

So the first lesson is that a blanket rule requiring a high school diploma to vote would mean substantial levels of democratic representation for many historically disadvantaged groups. But some groups would see their representation levels plummet; for instance, the American Amish tend to quit school after the eighth grade. And in Canada, members of the First Nations on average have a high school graduation rate of 38%, according to the Chiefs Assembly on Education.[6]

Toward the end of this chapter, I consider ways to address these important cases. And since I'm suggesting only 10% less democracy, a blanket high school diploma voting requirement for all voting would be bad in those cases. I'll keep the high school diploma voting requirement as a benchmark, a way to focus on the value of informed voters, but it's *not* a universal recommendation.

How Many Conspiracy Theorists Does It Take to Cripple a Democracy?

> From Plato to [John Stuart] Mill it has been argued that education and "intelligence" are preconditions for political rights.
>
> Ludvig Beckman

What would likely happen to government quality if only those with a high school diploma could vote? Here we have quite a lot of data, because public opinion polls typically ask about a respondent's highest education level. And the data are unambiguous: the more educated a person is, the more likely she is to know something about what the government is doing. She's more likely to have actual facts in mind and less likely to believe urban legends and conspiracy theories.

First, at the most basic level, those who are more educated are more likely to know what the government actually is. In one relevant study, public opinion researcher Vincenzo Memoli of the Università degli Studi di Catania looked at Italian survey data from the early 2000s.[7] Memoli's study measured political knowledge by asking Italian citizens questions like the name of the Italian prime minister (about two-thirds of Italians got that right) and if they could identify which political parties were on the left and which were on the right (about six-sevenths of Italians answered correctly, a little better). Memoli assembled the answers from these questions to give each respondent a total political knowledge score of 0 to 9. In his sample taken in 2001, for people with a college degree, the average score was 7.7. For people who had finished only elementary school, the average score was 4.7; for those who finished middle school, 5.3; and for high school graduates, 6.7. These differences are large compared to another difference that is always salient in Italian politics: the difference between northern Italians and southern Italians. In northern Italy the average political knowledge score was 6.0, and in southern Italy it was 5.2.

The educated are also less likely to believe in conspiracy theories. Of course, what counts as a "conspiracy theory" is a matter of debate. If all it takes to be a conspiracy theorist is to believe that government leaders sometimes don't tell you everything about how they make their decisions, well, then, sign me up. But if it means—well, let's turn it over to psychologist Jan-Willem Van Prooijen of VU Amsterdam, who presented people across the Netherlands with a number of statements that had to be graded on a 1 to 7 scale.[8] A 1 meant it was very unlikely to be true, and 7 meant it was "very plausible" or (in one of his studies, as he phrased it) "very likely" to be true. Here are some of the statements:

1. "People never really landed on the moon."

2. "Radiation of mobile phones is bad for our health. Both telecom companies and the government know this but keep the evidence a secret."

3. "The financial crisis was caused deliberately by bankers, for personal profit."

4. "The British Royal family was behind the murder of Princess Diana."

5. "Politicians are frequently being bribed by major companies or interest groups."

He then averaged the scores, yielding a number between 1 and 7.

Try taking this version of the test yourself and calculate your own average score. On this quiz, I got an average of 1.2, since in some ways campaign donations and soft promises of future jobs for retiring politicians are a lot like bribes. In Van Prooijen's first study, the average score was 4, and in his second study, the average was 3. But the standard deviation was 1 in both cases, which roughly means that any two random people in the first study typically had scores that differed by one, and two-thirds of the people in the study likely had a score of between 3 and 5. That's a pretty big range. So a lot of Dutch survey respondents—not Amsterdam college students, but instead people who live across the Netherlands—believe a lot of conspiracy theories are pretty plausible. And just as important, there's a wide range of variation.

So what predicts the variation in conspiracy beliefs? Two major psychological traits appear to matter: a feeling of powerlessness and a belief that most of life's big problems have simple solutions (an example statement of the latter is, "With the right policies, most problems in society are easy to solve"). But a reasonably good predictor of these two traits turns out to be education level. People with more education tend to think life's problems are harder to solve, and they feel more in control of their lives, which perhaps helps explain why they are less likely to turn to conspiracy theories as explanations to life's puzzling events.

How much did a lack of education by itself help predict belief in conspiracies? Van Prooijen's study of people across the Netherlands—again, a sample of the adult Dutch population—found that if you compared people who had an elementary school education versus a high school diploma or, equivalently, a high school diploma versus a community college diploma, the difference in conspiracy support was about three-quarters on that same 1 to 7 scale.

This isn't a claim that education *causes* less acceptance of conspiracy theories. That's not my claim at all, although it may well be part of the story. I emphasize merely a forecasting claim, a prediction claim: on election day, the voters who walk into the voting booth with less than a high school education will be noticeably more likely than other citizens to believe that the oil companies have a way to make energy free and they're just keeping it a secret to protect their profits.

One immediate lesson for supporters of democracy: if, like many other policy watchers, you think that most problems in society are actually hard to solve rather than easy to solve, you might appreciate having more voters who agree with you. And more education is a moderately strong predictor of less belief in conspiracies. Furthermore, if it's reasonable to be worried about having too many voters who hold too many far-fetched views about the death of Princess Diana, we should also be worried about having too many voters with poorly informed views on mundane policy issues. It's not only that the least educated are the most likely to fall for conspiracy theories. Perhaps even worse, they're more likely to fall for bad economic ideas.

My George Mason colleague Bryan Caplan conclusively documented in his famed book *The Myth of the Rational Voter* that the least educated are the most likely to support policies that are largely rejected by academic economists: higher taxes on imported goods, rent control, and tougher government-enforced rules that make it harder for firms to fire workers, to name just a few.[9] As Princeton's Blinder puts it in *Advice and Dissent*, "A more economically literate public would be a blessing."[10]

It's likely no surprise that the least educated are most likely to disagree with experts in economics; they're more likely than the educated to disagree with experts in medicine and history as well! Good thinking about social policy is hard, and it means carefully considering a wide variety of possible causes, considering both the direct and indirect effects of government action. It also helps to be at least casually familiar with the great body of real-world evidence on policy issues.

The democracies of today in the rich countries do not have education tests, but they frequently enforce mental competence tests, barring many individuals with intellectual disabilities from voting. The European Union Agency for Fundamental Rights has a useful, easy-to-read booklet that both (apparently) rejects the morality of these suffrage restrictions and yet makes it clear just how they work and why some countries have these restrictions on the right to vote. They explain it this way:

> In some countries in Europe, people with mental health problems are not allowed to vote.
>
> This is discrimination.
>
> Discrimination is when one person or a group of people are not treated in a fair way and do not have the same rights as everybody else. . . .
>
> In some countries [in Europe] people with mental health problems or intellectual disabilities can vote and take part in government. . . .
>
> In other countries they cannot.
>
> This is because the law says you cannot marry, buy a house, or look after your own money, so you cannot vote. These countries are:

Belgium	Lithuania
Bulgaria	Latvia
Czech Republic	Luxembourg
Denmark	Malta
Estonia	Poland
Germany	Portugal
Greece	Romania
Hungary	Slovakia

In some other countries, a doctor or judge decides if each person with mental health problems or intellectual disabilities can vote. These countries are:

Estonia	Malta
Cyprus	Slovenia
France	Spain[11]

Since many affluent democracies already take it for granted that some minimum level of life competence is a requirement for voting—that if "you cannot marry, buy a house, or look after your own money," then "you cannot vote"—then it's reasonable to debate where that competence cutoff should be set. Let's consider raising the cutoff.

Every serious theorist of democracy wrestles with the issue of voter competence, and to my reading, when the great writers make their cases for universal (or "universal") suffrage, they sound as if they're whistling past the graveyard, hoping no one will call them out for the strained reasoning required to conclude that every single adult can make a useful contribution to the national political debate. The case for political equality in the voting booth cannot be based on equal voter competence or even on nearly-equal voter competence. The much-less-educated in Italy are much less likely to know the name of the prime minister, and the much-less-educated in the Netherlands are much more likely to believe that the first human to step on the moon, Neil Armstrong, was a liar and a fraud.[12] Nearly-equal voter competence is a lie we should stop telling each other.

Balancing Alleged Human Rights

> The right to vote [in a free state] is enough to impose on me the
> duty to learn about public affairs, regardless of how weak might be
> the influence of my voice on them.
>
> Jean-Jacques Rousseau

If one wants to consider an alternative to the universal right to vote for all adults, then it's time to consider the wisdom of Georgetown

University philosopher Jason Brennan, who in a series of articles and an extremely useful book, *Against Democracy*, has made the case for *epistocracy*, rule by the informed.[13] Brennan is arguing for far greater reforms than I'm encouraging here. He's making the philosopher's case that a massive push toward allowing only the most informed to vote is within the range of reason. But along the way, he makes an important argument that matters for us: if one believes in the universal right to vote, one must balance that right against a universal right to have competent government. I personally don't believe that human rights exist in any meaningful sense—the utilitarian philosopher Jeremy Bentham put it best when he said rights were "nonsense on stilts"—but those who do believe in rights should be persuaded by Brennan's case.

Brennan notes that it's pointless to argue about what rights people can demand from their government unless those same people have a government competent enough to deliver on most of its promises. An abstract right to the freedom of speech is meaningless unless there's a government capable of keeping a promise not to ban controversial speech. Plenty of constitutions throughout the world make abstract promises that aren't ever kept. The most famous example might be in the Soviet constitutions, including the 1977 edition, which absurdly promised that "citizens of the USSR are guaranteed freedom of speech, of the press, and of assembly, meetings, street processions and demonstration."

But it's not just evil governments that make false promises. The world's most incompetent governments make outrageous promises of rights—promises that are routinely broken because the government isn't able to keep those promises, including the promised right to health care. A team of public health researchers at UCLA and McGill University collected data on the rights to health care set forth in dozens of constitutions around the world. They coded some versions of the right to health care as mere aspirations—boilerplate language about national goals—but other versions of the right to health care as true government guarantees. One concrete example:

Constitutional articles that unequivocally protected health rights or phrased them as a duty or obligation of the state were coded as guaranteed rights. Thus . . . in Venezuela [Const. Bolivarian Republic of Venezuela, 1999 (amended to 2009), art. 83], "[h]ealth is a fundamental social right" and the responsibility of the State, which shall guarantee it as part of the right to life.[14]

Even before the horrifying collapse of the Venezuelan health care system in the mid-2010s, the system had done a poor job guaranteeing this "part of the right to life." For instance, the maternal mortality rate in Venezuela has hovered a little above 90 maternal deaths per 100,000 live births, while the European Union nations have a rate of about 8 per 100,000. The guaranteed right to health, at least for mothers giving birth, is worth much less in Venezuela than it is in the EU.

If rights exist—to health, to freedom of speech, to a fair trial— then people hold a right to a government competent enough to provide those rights. One important ingredient in a competent government, says Brennan, is a reasonably informed, reasonably intelligent set of rulers. And in a democracy, ordinary citizens are, in an important sense, the rulers.

The most cynical supporters of the universal right to vote might take precisely the opposite position. They might support such a right precisely because they believe that voting *doesn't* change things. To these cynics, an equal right to vote gives people equal dignity in the same sense that in children's T-ball leagues, every child has a right to hit the ball. In the cynical view, the game of voting doesn't matter in the first place, so we should just let everybody play. Participation medals all around!

But the game does matter—at least the game of voting in a democracy. New voters mean new policies. This is a claim for which there's abundant evidence in historical and statistical research. A few examples:

- Irish immigrants to American cities in the nineteenth century changed the political landscape in those cities, creating new political machines and new, often more personal (some would say corrupt) norms of governance. The short book *Plunkitt of Tammany Hall* is the finest anthropological piece of evidence on this subject.

- Extending the franchise to women in the United States and across Europe in the nineteenth and early twentieth centuries appears to have caused government spending on childhood education and health care to increase.[15]

- Since women have long been more supportive of tariff barriers than men, the women's suffrage movement appears to have exacerbated the global turn away from free trade in the early twentieth century. Polling data from the United States, historical evidence from Britain, and the pattern of changes in tariff rates across dozens of countries support this claim.[16]

Nearly every study that investigates whether extending the franchise to new groups has had an effect on government policy finds that the answer is a clear yes. What's more, in the widely studied case of women's suffrage, policy changed in just the way you'd expect if you knew the average policy differences between women and men. Men worry less about health issues compared to women on average—in the rich countries, men go to the doctor much less, and spend smaller fractions of their income on health-related matters—so it's little surprise that when groups with differing views in their private lives enter the public sphere as voters, they bring different issues into the voting booth. And governments respond to those differing concerns.

This point is perhaps obvious, but it is worth reiterating: The reason to consider restricting the right to vote to those with a bare minimum level of education isn't for some grand metaphysical reason. The purity of the sacred voting booth won't be polluted if a voter without a high school diploma enters therein. Instead, the reason to consider restricting the vote to those with a bare minimum of education is that good policy genuinely matters, and it matters so much that we should do more to raise the probability of getting good policy. Raising the average information level of voters by truncating the lower tail of the education distribution is a practical way to raise the probability of getting good policy.

Many people will agree that the least-informed voters hurt government quality at least a little, but they'll be reluctant to create a blanket lifetime ban on voting just because someone was a little lazy in high school. And as noted earlier, some cultural groups tend to have quite low graduation rates. So let's consider some modifications. The voter education requirement could be "high school diploma or equivalent," where "equivalent" could vary country by country. In the United States, the GED (General Equivalency Diploma) exam is widely considered a good substitute for a high school diploma, even if earned years after the typical age at graduation. A minimum college entrance exam score—perhaps at the 10th percentile of the score distribution—could be also an alternative to meeting the voter education requirement. Many nations might offer an additional path to the right to vote: military service. In Robert Heinlein's science-fiction novel *Starship Troopers*, the right to vote was restricted solely to those who had served in the military.[17] "Service Guarantees Citizenship" was the slogan. In practice, this wouldn't create many additional voters in the United States, since a high school diploma or GED is a requirement for current military service, and the military's de facto IQ test, the Armed Forces Qualifying Test, tends to screen out individuals at the bottom tail of the intelligence distribution. But other countries might have other rules and might want to create a path to voting eligibility for those who are unable to meet the standard voter education requirement. "At 20 years of age the will reigns; at 30 the wit; at 40 the judgment." So said Benjamin Franklin in the 1741 edition of *Poor Richard's Almanac*.[18] Inspired by this aphorism, a nation could decide to give everyone the right to vote at age forty. For people who live in the rich countries, that means almost everyone gets the right to vote eventually. It may be difficult to measure whether judgment—a subjective concept—improves with age, but the study of Italian voter knowledge already discussed showed that voters in the forty-five to sixty-four age range knew quite a bit more about politics than those in the eighteen to twenty-four age range. Likewise, a study of Canadians by Daniel Stockemer and François Rocher, government scholars at the University of Ottawa, reported based on survey data that "younger individuals are more politically illiterate than older generations by a [substantial] margin."[19]

Age restrictions for those with low levels of education do have some precedent. Legal scholar Giorgio Del Vecchio, emeritus professor at the University of Rome, noted that "the [Italian] law of June 30, 1912, granted the vote to illiterate people, but only on the condition that they had reached their thirtieth year or had fulfilled their military obligations."[20]

Perhaps the Italians of a little over a century ago had a practical path to 10% less democracy, and perhaps they erred when, six years later in 1918, in the aftermath of the Great War, they dropped that universal male voting age down to twenty-one. It was only four years later, in 1922, that Benito Mussolini was elected as the nation's youngest and worst prime minister.

Education-Based Gerrymandering

As we've seen, there's more than one way to tilt the scales to give more educated citizens a slightly larger voice in a democracy. Here's another. In countries where legislators have territory-based districts—a member of Parliament from Kensington or a congress-woman from Columbus, Ohio, for instance—these districts could be made 10% smaller than average when the district has an above-average education level. And similarly, districts could be made 10% larger than average if the district has a below-average education level. Ultimately this would lead to about a 10% difference in the number of districts held by those with above-average levels of education.

Consider this example of what I call smart redistricting: 1,000 voters, where initially there are 10 voters per district, for a total of 100 legislators in the national assembly. If the districts with above-average

educations are made 10% smaller, then instead of having 50 legislators representing 10 voters each, they'll now have 55 legislators
representing 9 voters each (I'm rounding for simplicity). And in
the districts with below-average education levels, they'll have the
remaining 45 legislators who each represent 11 voters in the national
assembly. Everyone still gets represented, everyone still gets to vote,
and yet the national assembly would give a touch more weight to
those who can correctly answer the question, "What will probably
happen to the unemployment rate if we double the minimum wage?"

Less Democracy: The Path of Inaction

> Voting can legitimately be restricted, however, on the basis of citi-
> zenship, mental capacity, or a criminal record.
>
> United Nations Women Watch

One of my favorite jazz pieces, by Les McCann and Eddie Harris, has
a title that I call the economist's question: "Compared to what?" The
voting reforms I've suggested are about making concrete changes
compared to the status quo. Here I want to suggest another way to
improve voter education levels: by inaction rather than action.

Here I have a pro-epistocracy voting reform that involves doing
nothing at all: don't restore voting rights to felons. This issue of whether
felons should be allowed to vote has been salient in the United States
in recent years as the rise in mass incarceration in the 1980s and 1990s
created millions more convicted, imprisoned, and released felons than
ever before. In the United States, and to some degree in Belgium,
Italy, Greece, and Luxembourg, convicted felons are stripped of their
voting rights even after their release from prison.[21] The rights-based
argument for doing so is that felons have violated the social contract
in an important way and have thereby lost the right to vote.

Again, I'm not one for rights-based arguments as a rule—nonsense
on stilts and all—so let's turn instead to an outcome-based argument.
On average, felons have substantially lower education levels than non-
felons. A 2003 Bureau of Justice Statistics (BJS) report shows just

how low the average education levels of America's incarcerated citizens are. Caroline Wolf Harlow, a Bureau of Justice Statistics statistician, reports: "About 41% of inmates in the Nation's State and Federal prisons and local jails in 1997 and 31% of probationers had not completed high school or its equivalent. In comparison, 18% of the general population age 18 or older had not finished the 12th grade."[22]

Those numbers make the education gap between the incarcerated and other Americans look smaller than it is because the inmate statistics included those words "or its equivalent." Twenty-three percent of inmates had a GED, so taking them out of the mix means the high school diploma gap between the incarcerated and the rest of the population is now a gap between the 64% of prisoners who didn't get at least a high school diploma and the 18% of the general population who didn't get at least that far. That's a gap of more than 40 percentage points between the incarcerated and the general population.

If there's already a soft, incomplete social consensus that felons have a relatively weak claim to voting rights, let's do what we can to strengthen that consensus. Every nudge, every small push, every tweak that we can make to slightly raise the skill level of voters is a step in the direction of more competent government. And remember, lots of political theorists believe we have a right to competent government. Compared to giving American, Italian, Greek, Luxembourger, and Belgian felons the right to vote, doing nothing is an important step on the path to 10% less democracy.

Upper Houses into Human Capital Houses: Senators into Sapientors

> The uneducated man or the man with limited education is a different political actor from the man who has achieved a higher level of education.
>
> Gabriel Almond and Sidney Verba

Historically in English-speaking countries, the upper houses of a nation's legislature—the House of Lords in the United Kingdom, the Senates in Canada and the United States—have been bodies assigned an entirely different and more openly elitist role than the lower house. The British House of Commons has been designed for over a century to represent "The People." Full stop. By contrast, the House of Lords was designed to represent the voice of the nation's elite—the Lords Temporal and the Lords Spiritual—though the boundaries of that elite have drifted over the centuries. The House of Lords was long a tool for representing the hereditary nobility and the Church of England, though it has drifted over to a membership with far more lifetime appointments—life peerages, of former prime ministers, for instance—and as time passes, it has become more like a mere advisory committee, with little real power to stop legislation. But although the powers of the House of Lords have weakened, the underlying principle—that the nation's elites should have a concrete voice in government—is worth keeping in mind.

In Germany, members of the upper house, the Bundesrat, are appointed by their regional governments and have no term at all; they serve until they are fired by their regional governments. By contrast, members of the lower house in Germany, the Bundestag, have four-year terms. In the United States, as we've seen, senators have a six-year term, compared to two years in the lower house. Clearly, governments have been trying to solve various political problems with the differing appointment and election methods used in these upper houses. Upper houses frequently have longer terms, but beyond that, there's little consensus on what their job should be.

I suggest a possible new role for a nation's upper house: it could become a Sapientum, to coin a term—a council of the wise, rather than a Senate, a word with Latin roots that suggest a council of the old. And the path to converting a Senate into a Sapientum would come from changing who votes for its members, who votes for its Sapientors. The citizens who choose among potential Sapientors could be required to have, on average, substantially more education, more skill, more human capital than those who vote for the members of the lower houses. To vote in the Sapientum election, you'd have to meet some sort of education requirement.

This may be the most practical way to implement a modest move in the direction of epistocracy. Everyone with a current right to vote gets to vote in elections for the lower house and for the head of state, but only those with a college degree or equivalent can vote in elections to the upper house. Our cultures largely reject the value of tradition and heritage as a reason to make appointments to the upper body of the legislature, so a House of Lords will not work, if it ever did. But we still respect the idea that some people know more than others. That truth can be the foundation of elections to the Sapientum.

As with the high school diploma voting requirement, there should be room to widen the standards a bit—some well-chosen loopholes, so that it's not "a college diploma" requirement but instead "college diploma or equivalent." What might the "or equivalent" path be to qualify for voting for the upper house? Whatever a nation's citizens consider a good substitute. A master plumber or journeyman pipefitter, a certified sommelier, anyone with five years in a craft trade: these might all be plausible metrics that capture a degree of knowledge and insight. Military service could be another path. And again, recall that the goal isn't to grant individuals the sacred right to participate in the legislative process; the goal is to get better policy outcomes. Yes, any precise cutoff for who can and cannot vote will be arbitrary, leaving some unworthies inside the voting booth and some worthies outside. But some nations already do the same when allowing those who commit misdemeanor crimes to vote while stripping voting rights away from those who commit felonies—since the decision of whether to charge a defendant with a felony or a misdemeanor is up to the raw discretion of a prosecutor. Similarly, resident aliens can live in a country for years, decades, and yet small administrative details can determine who gets full citizenship, including the right to vote, and who gets mere residency rights. And age cutoffs forbid those who die young from ever voting.

Recognizing the arbitrariness of the voting restrictions we already have is the first step to being open to creating one more arbitrary voting restriction. But this arbitrary cutoff—the Sapientum cutoff—could create an entire branch of the legislature chosen by citizens substantially more informed than average. A branch of the legislature that was explicitly epistocratic would be likely to make wiser, more farsighted, more informed voting decisions as a result.

And, by the way, Ireland has already embraced elements of the Sapientum. Its upper house, the Seanad Éireann, has sixty members, and of those sixty, three are elected solely by graduates of the University of Dublin (effectively the same institution as Trinity College Dublin) and another three are elected solely by graduates of the National University of Ireland. The Seanad Éireann is weak—it can only delay legislation, not defeat it—but with 10% of the seats chosen by graduates of elite universities, Ireland has found its own way toward 10% more epistocracy. If Ireland, with a population of a little under 5 million, gives two great universities 10% of the seats in the upper house, a proportional plan for the United States might reserve 10% of all Senate seats for elections where the only eligible voters would be graduates of America's 140 best universities. Ireland's Sapientum-lite is well worth considering.

The Transitional Gains Trap: A Barrier to Epistocracy

Gordon Tullock, my late colleague at GMU's Center for Study of Public Choice, once tried to explain why genuinely good reform proposals are so hard to implement.[23] He said a big reason that it's hard to enact good reforms, ones that grow society's economic pie, is that the old, bad rules have already created a group of insiders who sacrificed and struggled to do well under those old, bad rules. And they're afraid of reform because reform means their old sacrifices will have been for nothing. And perhaps just as important, those insiders can make a pretty sympathetic plea to the rest of us to let them keep the little fiefdom they've created. The insiders make a good case. Even a good reform will certainly create losers, so is it really worth it to create certain losers in the mere hope that the reform works out okay?

New York taxi drivers are a great example. Economists had complained for decades about New York City's bizarre method for restricting the supply of taxis. The city requires anyone who wants to drive a taxi to purchase one of a fixed supply of taxi cab medallions, a literal medal that says you have a right to drive a taxi in the city. At their peak, these medallions were worth a million dollars each according to economist Mark Perry of the American Enterprise Institute.[24] Economists and transit activists alike encouraged the city to expand the supply of medallions or, even better, to stop requiring drivers to own a medallion. Instead, let the forces of supply and demand determine the number of cabs in the city.

But you can imagine one sympathetic group of New Yorkers who would fight against massively increasing the supply of medallions: taxicab drivers who already own a medallion! They've already sweated and sacrificed to come up with the half-million dollars or more to buy a medallion, and now some professor wants to declare their investments worthless! How's that for justice?

And the taxicab driver makes a pretty strong case. Tullock's "transitional gains trap" is really better thought of as a "transitional losses trap." The fact that good reforms usually require some people to lose out on some investment they've made in good faith means that good reform proposals start off with strong, sympathetic opponents to reform. Hair stylists opposing the end of cosmetology licensing, tax accountants opposing tax simplification proposals, professors with tenure fighting against ending guaranteed jobs for life: in each case, an insider who spent a long time making an expensive investment is being told that that investment is going to collapse in value, all for the sake of the so-called common good.

This is a lot like the problem we face with any pro-epistocracy voting reform: people feel entitled to the right to vote that they grew up with, the right that they were raised on. And other citizens feel that their less educated neighbors shouldn't have a right stripped away. So is there a practical way to handle the transitional losses trap?

Here's one simple way: don't restrict the voting rights of anyone who had a right to vote the day the reform was enacted. Phase in the change over time, making the voting restrictions entirely forward looking. Change the future batch of voters, not the current batch. This is known in the legislative world as grandfathering—letting people keep the benefits they currently have so reformers can avoid having to fight entrenched interests. Other phase-in paths are possible—like retaining the full voting rights for anyone at least ten years old as of the date of enactment—but the principle is clear: people hate giving up things they have, but they are less likely to miss things they never had in the first place.

That means that I could have given this chapter a different title: "This Chapter Does Not Apply to Your Generation."

Avoiding Epistocratic Tyranny

With any of these voting restrictions I suggest in this chapter, it's possible to go too far. One should always be wondering whether any targeted restriction on the right to vote will leave a minority group at the mercy of the majority—that was James Madison's *Federalist No. 51* concern about the tyranny of the majority. And when a minority is at the mercy of a majority in a democracy, persecution, hunger, and premature death loom.

It's obviously true that representation matters. If an ethnic or cultural group is overwhelmingly excluded from political life, then the very worst outcomes become possible. And the one thing democracy clearly has going for it is that it helps to avoid the very worst outcomes. That's one reason I focus on more modest reforms that slightly tilt the weight of voter voices in one direction or another.

That means, among other things, that I'm presuming that people who just barely graduate from high school have a lot in common with those who don't graduate—and since those barely graduated citizens would still be able to vote, they'll tend to represent most of the views and interests of the nongraduates who largely wouldn't be able to vote. If governments vote to explicitly ban high school dropouts from receiving health care or disaster relief or disability insurance payments, then my voter restriction proposal will be a failure. But one should weigh the low probability of those bad effects of voter restriction against the benefits of a better-informed electorate, of political campaigns where the candidates only need to appeal to the second-lowest common denominator. Then, if the probability of a bad outcome from voter restriction appears high, don't restrict the right to vote.

An Aside: Buckley's Phone Book

The late conservative intellectual William F. Buckley once famously said that he'd rather be governed by the first two thousand names in the Boston phone book than by the two thousand members of the faculty of Harvard University. The TV interview where he repeats his famous saying is great fun, and I recommend giving it a look. It's a great quote for demonstrating fellow feeling with the common citizen. But was Buckley right? I'll leave you to come up with your own answer, but I'll give you mine: rather than be governed by the masses of Boston or by the professors of Harvard, I'd far rather be governed by the engineering faculty of MIT.

Should Surgeons Operate on Their Relatives?

I gave this chapter its title in the hopes that readers would stand back and look at the important topic of who votes with some emotional distance, some cool objectivity. Important decisions often require emotional detachment: The American Medical Association's official statement on a related topic says, "Physicians generally should not treat themselves or members of their immediate families. Professional objectivity may be compromised when an immediate family member or the physician is the patient; the physician's personal feelings may unduly influence his or her professional medical judgment, thereby interfering with the care being delivered."[25]

Perhaps, even after considering the case for modest pro-epistocracy reforms, you'll come away thinking, "Some good points, but our country shouldn't do that." And well, maybe your country shouldn't. But maybe somebody else's country should. And maybe, if a few countries raise the voting age to twenty-five or let only college graduates vote for members of the upper house or gerrymander slightly smaller districts for the highly educated, you can watch and see how that turns out. Again, with some cool, emotional detachment.

In the past century and a half, the rich democracies tried the universal franchise, and while its record hasn't been an unmitigated disaster, it could certainly be improved. Small- to medium-sized steps in the direction of epistocracy will likely improve policy choices at little or no cost to the quality of life of the less educated. Indeed, if the epistocrats are right, the less educated are likely to be better off from the change—they'll be living under more competent rulers than before.

And in this chapter especially, I want to draw attention to an underlying theme of every policy proposal I make in this book. If any policy reform I suggest violates your personal morality, then don't push for its enactment. But first, discover the cost of your morality. It may be more expensive than you think.

Coda: Heinlein's Quadratic Metaphor

The science-fiction novelist Robert Heinlein thought quite a lot about how to improve democracy. As noted earlier, in *Starship Troopers* only members of the military could vote—service guaranteed citizenship. But he had other ideas. He once imagined a government

> that required a bare minimum of intelligence and education—e.g., step into the polling booth and find that the computer has generated a new quadratic equation just for you. Solve it, the computer unlocks the voting machine, you vote. But get a wrong answer and the voting machine fails to unlock, a loud bell sounds, a red light goes on over the booth—and you slink out, face red, you having just proved yourself too stupid and/or ignorant to take part

in the decisions of grownups. Better luck next election! No lower age limit in this system—smart 12-yr-old girls vote every election while some of their mothers—and fathers—decline to be humiliated twice.[26]

A quadratic equation can take the form of an upside-down U, an inverted parabola, shaped just like the Laffer curve. Recall that a Laffer curve shows that if you start the tax rate off at zero and increase it from there, you'll generate more tax revenue for a while, but eventually you'll reach the peak. If the tax rate rises above that level—the top of the Laffer curve—you'll push so many people into the black market or early retirement or accounting games that the government will start losing revenue.

The benefits and costs of widespread citizen voting might be another Laffer curve type of relationship. If voting is purely a universal human right, and not at all a means to an end of good governance, then restricting the vote to the highly educated would be a terrible voting method, and expanding the franchise more will yield ever-greater moral benefits at no cost to society. But if the economist's usual story that life is about trade-offs holds true here, then a wider voting franchise has benefits for a while—for instance, by avoiding famine or reducing the risk of government-backed domestic massacres or by creating a greater feeling of social inclusion. But too wide a franchise will eventually have important costs—in particular, a lower level of average voter information, which spurs politicians to pander to voters with a narrower, weaker knowledge base. The net benefits of expanding the franchise beyond the highly educated are probably very high, but we should try to find the top of the suffrage Laffer curve, the peak of the body politic's parabola.

We'd be foolish to take Heinlein's suggestion for voting reform literally, but we should certainly take it seriously.

6 Bondholders as a Separate and Coequal Branch of Government

I used to think if there was reincarnation, I wanted
to come back as the president or the pope or a .400
baseball hitter. But now I want to come back as the bond
market. You can intimidate everybody.

JAMES CARVILLE
Political adviser to President Clinton

DEMOCRACIES ALREADY HAVE A STRONG CHECK on the power of citizens: the national debt. It was Alexander Hamilton, the first U.S. treasury secretary, who made the case in a letter to financier Robert Morris: "A national debt if it is not excessive will be to us a national blessing; it will be powerfull cement of our union."[1]

I can't agree with each step in Hamilton's reasoning; for example, later in the same letter, he contended that the high taxes needed to repay the debt would get lazy Americans to work more. But Hamilton was right that the national debt would be a "cement [to America's] union." One reason: investors who purchase a nation's debt have a strong interest in the long-term financial stability of the nation. Recall that government debt is typically referred to as bonds, and people who invest in that debt are known as bondholders. Informally, bondholders treat the government the same way they treat any other business they invest in: they want the government to run a profit, keeping expenses low enough and revenues high enough so that there's enough left over to repay the bondholders—with interest.

If there's one critique of democracy that has resonated through the ages, it's that democracies have a hard time focusing on the future. But the pressure that bondholders put on governments can be a powerful force to encourage governments to give some thought for the morrow. Bondholders are an important and useful check on the potentially reckless behavior of governments, a check that democracy theorists almost entirely ignore. This chapter will help rectify that omission.

Individuals, banks, and investment funds that hold your government's debt (also known as sovereign debt) are already exerting a force on how your country is run. I claim that your nation would be better off if that role were formalized. Long-term government bondholders—investors holding maturities of, say, ten years or longer—should be given an explicit advisory role in modern democracies as a check on the shortsighted, impulsive, frequently ignorant electorate. If your government really gets into financial trouble, its present and potential future investors are going to have a seat at the table anyway, even if that table is located behind closed doors in a government conference room. Let's bring that conference table out into the open. Let's hold some of those meetings with long-term bondholders before the fiscal crisis strikes. That just might prevent the crisis from ever happening.

Alexander Hamilton: A Friend of Bondholder-as-Monitor

> Those who are most commonly creditors of a nation, are, generally speaking, enlightened men.
>
> Alexander Hamilton

Our first and still most important secretary of the treasury, Alexander Hamilton, didn't just provide an offhand quip about the merits of a sovereign debt: he built a new nation's entire fiscal policy around it. The most important element of that policy was that he decided that the U.S. government should frequently issue debt, precisely in order to see how financial markets felt about the government's financial stability.[2]

Recall that a bond is like a bank account where you pay money today in exchange for receiving a certain amount of money back in the future: So you might pay the U.S. government $90 today, and in return, the U.S. government would give you $100 five years from now. That would be a five-year bond, with a yield (i.e., an effective annual interest rate) of about 2% per year. So when governments raise money by borrowing, it's called "selling bonds." Getting money through bond issues is often a practical way of borrowing from the public. In 1997, musical artist David Bowie raised $55 million by is-suing what quickly became known as "Bowie Bonds"—bonds backed by royalties from his pre-1990 albums. Bowie used some of those bond proceeds to buy back the rights to other recordings he had made earlier in his career.[3] Selling bonds to dozens, even thousands or millions, of investors gives borrowers an alternative to going to banks: it cuts out the middleman and harnesses the power of market competition to push borrowing costs down.

At the same time, market competition means public disclosure: everyone can tell how you're doing. Often governments hold auc-tions to sell their bonds, and then sell the bonds to the highest bid-ders. That keeps the government's interest costs as low as possible. But the winning bid price instantly becomes public information, so it works a little like a public opinion poll but even more like a stock price. If investors today were willing to pay a high price for a right to, say, a hundred U.S. dollars five years from now, then that means people are reasonably confident they'll be repaid in full. If instead the government auctions off some bonds and the winning price is low, well, that's a sign people are thinking they might get repaid late, might get repaid half of what they were promised, or, in the worst case, might not get repaid at all.

And again, here's the crucial fact: the winning price—this real-time-referendum on the health of the government—is published openly and immediately. Many folk theories and formal theories of democracy assume that government insiders are managing expecta-tions, hiding uncomfortable facts, and spinning the truth day in and day out. But here, in the market for sovereign bonds, there's at least one clear fact, available for all to see: the market's judgment of your government's financial health. That's been true since 1790 in the United States, and it's currently best practice for all of the world's rich democracies. Governments are routinely issuing bonds—partly to finance new borrowing but mostly to repay old debt by issuing new debt (a practice known as rolling over the debt).

I can only assume that Lin-Manuel Miranda had a song about our first treasury secretary's deep understanding of the role of global financial elites ready to go for his hit musical *Hamilton*, but—alas—had to omit the song due to time constraints. Perhaps it went something like this, to the tune of The Doors's "Light My Fire":

> The time to obfuscate is through
> Investor mood is growing dire
> They say our figures are untrue
> The global pool of money's drier
> Full disclosure: Let's a-spire
> Full disclosure: Let's a-spire

Why do governments routinely allow such a glaring light to shine on their financial condition? For the same reason moviemakers usually allow movie critics to see even their mediocre movies a few days before release: because if you're hiding your product, it's a sign you know your product is terrible. And investors, like moviegoers, stay away from products that look terrible.

Cautious Money Makes a Candid Monitor

> President Clinton visits Ottawa tomorrow, but all the Canadian papers are talking about is the visit they just had from the other superpower—the Man from Moody's.
>
> Thomas Friedman

There's a bad idea out there, all too popular: "A nation that prints its own currency can never default on its debt." After all, story goes, a sovereign government can always print enough paper currency to "pay back" the government's bondholders. Here, the quotation marks around "pay back" really are ironic quotes, almost scare quotes.

Yes, the famous bond rating agencies—Standard & Poor's, Moody's, and Fitch—all treat such hyperinflation repayments as genuine repayments. So if the United Kingdom got into financial trouble and started printing British pounds on a photocopier, setting off a hyperinflation—well, as long as the government repays its debt, even with nearly worthless hyperinflated money, the debt counts as repaid, both legally and in the eyes of the rating agencies. But normal investors don't fall for that fiction. They know that if they're repaid in hyperinflated currency, that's default by another name. Strangely, hyperinflation-driven default is known as "soft default," a bizarre use of language since, as we'll see below, normal bond-rating-agency recognized default is usually a better deal for investors.

Investors don't believe the fiction that hyperinflated repayment is repayment, and so they run away from a nation's bonds if the nation looks as if it's running toward the printing press. When high inflation looms, bond prices plummet, and therefore interest rates on the bonds skyrocket. That higher interest rate isn't a gift. It represents the fact that most of the "gain" from holding the bond would be purely inflationary. If a government bond promising to pay $100 in a year is now selling at a price of $1 on the open market, that roughly 10,000% annual rate of return means that investors are worried that either the government isn't going to repay at all, or that if it does repay something called "one hundred dollars," those "dollars" a year from now won't be enough to buy a hyperinflated Big Mac.

Nobel laureate Christopher Sims made a related point in his Nobel lecture, "Paper Money."[4] Sims emphasized that the inflation-adjusted return on U.S. government debt has varied quite a lot over the decades. The biggest piece of bad news for U.S. bondholders since World War II was the unexpectedly high inflation of the 1970s. People who bought long-term U.S. government bonds in the early

1970s lost a lot of value. If you had lent (to give approximate figures) $100 to the United States in 1972 for ten years, you got back enough money when you were repaid a decade later to buy just $82 worth of goods. Yes, you would have been repaid "one hundred dollars" in 1982 plus interest, but since prices had nearly doubled over the decade, that sum of money bought 18% less than it did in 1972. The bondholders of the 1970s paid for the privilege of lending to the U.S. government, and that experience made investors cautious about lending to the U.S. government ever again.

By the late 1970s, after it became clear that U.S. government bondholders might get burned by high inflation, investors insisted on higher yields, higher interest rates, and so they paid lower prices for U.S. government debt. Those low prices were expensive for the government and its taxpayers. The government didn't have to just repay the money it borrowed; it had to repay investors enough to make up for the fear, the risk, that high inflation could happen again. This pattern continued through the 1980s and 1990s. Even in 1988, six years after inflation had dramatically (and, so far, persistently) fallen, investors were (effectively) paying $100 in 1988 and getting repaid $190 in inflation-adjusted buying power in 1998.[5] The global pool of money that chose to invest in America during the late 1980s and 1990s received a massive return on what turned out to be a safe, fairly low-inflation investment, in large part because the United States had burned its reputation in the high-inflation 1970s. It's expensive to rebuild a burned reputation.

The lesson from the U.S.'s flirtation with soft default in the 1970s? Global investors pay close attention to the economic health and wellbeing of governments. Interest rates on a government's sovereign debt are a useful tool for tracking the health of a nation's overall economy. Another useful tool is bond ratings from the major agencies. Around the world, bond ratings tend to move closely with the interest rates on a government's debt, and they're a convenient (though obviously imperfect) way to check out the wisdom and sustainability of a government's long-term policies. And while a nation and that nation's government aren't the same thing, good governments are more likely to have good economies. That's why I often require my macroeconomics students to check out the government bond ratings for multiple countries: to get a sense of who is running a tight ship and who is asleep at the wheel.

Sovereign Bondholders: Unelected Bureaucrats Overseeing the Global Pool of Money

These ratings aren't perfect predictors of the future, but perfection is not the standard for those of us who toil on this fallen earth. Instead, the ratings give us a sense of where things may be going, and they are a reminder that somebody out there is turning a clinical eye to your government's policies—somebody who isn't concerned with which political team is up and which team is down or which moral arguments are growing in popularity in your country. The bondholders, the rating agencies, and the global pool of money are interested in just one thing: whether your government will pay on time.

The detached view of the global investor shares something in common with the detached view of the unelected bureaucrat who runs an independent central bank, but the investor has something else going for him: he can walk away from your economy with a few strokes of the keyboard, dumping your bonds and moving on to safer havens. This detached view is useful in getting good advice, and while government finance ministries and treasury departments in the rich democracies aren't in the habit of openly asking potential bond investors for advice, they certainly do try to put on a good show for this global pool of money. For instance, in the mid-2000s, the Japanese finance ministry held a meeting at the Japan Club of New York, "pitching Japanese government bonds to U.S. investors in an effort to diversify the country's bondholder base. . . . [Vice Finance Minister for International Affairs Hiroshi] Watanabe said U.S. investors are interested in Japan's fiscal situation . . . and how the government plans to restore Japan's fiscal health."[6]

Sometimes these meetings become more routinized. In the Victorian era, British investors who held foreign sovereign debt created the Corporation of Foreign Bondholders (CFB). They offered advice to the nations they invested in, and their advice was well worth listening to if a nation wanted to be able to borrow again from these reasonably well-informed, affluent, risk-averse investors. The CFB was active for well over a century. Its annual reports are available on Stanford University's library website and demonstrate the long attention span of bondholders. The 1983 report noted that the CFB was still overseeing the repayment of debts originally owed by the Austro-Hungarian Empire, which dissolved after World War I. The CFB noted that the empire's debts were expected to be paid off, finally, in 1986.

The U.S. government had a similar organization, created under the auspices of President Franklin Roosevelt in the 1930s: the Foreign Bondholders Protective Council. Less successful than the CFB, it nominally existed at least as late as 2002, but has never held the reasonably high status that the CFB held for decades. By contrast, the Paris Club, "the major forum where creditor countries renegotiate official sector [e.g., government-to-government] debts," has had reasonably high international stature since its origin in 1956.[7] The Paris Club itself says that "conditionality" is one of its six guiding principles: "The Paris Club only negotiates debt restructurings with debtor countries that . . . have implemented and are committed to implementing reforms to restore their economic and financial situation, and . . . have a demonstrated track record of implementing reforms under an IMF program."[8]

The Paris Club doesn't have to create the reform program itself. Instead, it provides indebted countries with a strong financial incentive to "implement reforms to restore their economic and financial situation." It's a visible hand of discipline that encourages governments to focus on long-run financial sustainability. And obviously, one important way to improve long-run financial sustainability is to raise the borrower nation's productivity. Productive nations, like productive companies, find it easier to pay their bills. The Paris Club's disciplinary role obviously doesn't have to be motivated by altruism, but by focusing national governments on the ability to make payments over the long run, they're probably improving the lot of the average citizen. The visible hand of discipline foreshadows the invisible hand of higher productivity.

Note that the British Corporation of Foreign Bondholders, the U.S. Foreign Bondholders Protective Council, and the Paris Club were each designed by lenders looking to make their case to borrowers. My first proposal is different: I propose that borrowers themselves take the lead. The finance ministry of each rich democracy should design its own formal financial high council, inviting domestic and foreign bond investors (or, more realistically, their appointed representatives) to meet regularly and often openly with finance ministry and parliamentary officials.

A modern version in the U.S. case might be a Council of Treasury Bondholders, a formal organization where U.S. Treasury bondholders could share their collective views on U.S. economic policy, perhaps through nonbinding public resolutions where one dollar of bonds means one vote. Another approach would be the German model of corporate governance. In Germany, big banks are frequently major investors in the country's biggest private corporations, and those banks have routinely been given one or more seats on the boards of these corporations. Thus, in German corporations, the big lenders literally have a seat at the table. With just a few legal changes, the same could be true in cabinet meetings of the United States, the United Kingdom, Japan, or other debt-laden democracies.

If you're concerned that a few big bondholders—particularly foreign governments—could exercise too much political influence on such a council, then go ahead and include rules that state, for example, that neither a single investor nor any closely connected group of investors could hold more than 10% of the seats on the council. At least at the start, such a restriction would be natural as a nation tests the waters of what I call *investor-inclusive governance*, a version of the stakeholder theory of the state. But at the same time, keep in mind that the biggest investors certainly have a strong financial incentive to make sure the government can pay its debts. They're focused on the long run in a way that few voters are. And whatever worries one might have about allowing elite corporations or foreign agents a voice in the government, remember that those investors don't have to be perfect to be worth listening to; they just have to be better than your nation's voters. Again, it's the economists' question: "Compared to what?"

Options that other rich democracies might consider could include formal annual shareholder-style meetings between elected bondholder representatives and elected government officials, formal appointments of bondholder representatives to high-level finance ministry positions, or even handing bondholder representatives limited forms of veto power over economic policy actions. A soft veto, as in the current House of Lords, would be one model. A veto might delay enactment for a few weeks or perhaps send it back to the legislature for "one more vote, just to be sure you mean it."

Another option—one I find particularly practical—would be to grant the bondholder council a small number of seats in the upper house of the national legislature. The Sapientum of the previous chapter could create some space for government bondholders. Those elected by the more informed and those elected by the more patient would sit side by side, joint checks on the democratically elected lower house and the democratically elected executive. The number of seats that belonged to these bondholders would rise as the nation's ratio of government debt to national income rose. One more seat in the upper house for every 10% increase in the debt-to-income ratio would focus the mind of governments that borrowed heavily and would tend to bring a more farsighted perspective to government deliberations. In many governing traditions, the upper house is designed to be the house of wisdom, and while wisdom may be hard to come by in politics, long-run vision is a damn good substitute.

A Government Powerful Enough to Give You Everything You Want Will Never Get a Loan

Some might object to the idea of admitting bondholders to the councils of power. The sovereignty of the state, some might say, requires that the state stand apart, independent of its financiers. And if that's too lofty an aspiration, practical politics seems to offer the same lesson: the state really *can* say no whenever it likes, can't it? In a democracy, after all, aren't the citizens supposed to be the bosses? Or at the very least, in a modern nation-state, isn't the government the party with the guns, with a monopoly on the legitimate use of force? And at the crudest level, wasn't Mao right when he said that political power grows out of the barrel of a gun?

All of these claims are so incomplete that they are wrong. Prosperity comes from the ability to coordinate various inputs—physical labor, capital, human minds—in creative and useful ways. And often a government needs to borrow some inputs that will pay off later. It needs lenders. Indeed, the government needs lenders so much that it knows that even if it is tempted to default today, it will try to resist that temptation because it knows it will need to borrow again in the near future. Hamilton talked about this need to build a reputation as a good lender in his *First Report on the Public Credit*:

> And as on the one hand, the necessity for borrowing in particular emergencies cannot be doubted, so on the other, it is equally evident, that to be able to borrow upon good terms, it is essential that the credit of a nation should be well established.

> For when the credit of a country is in any degree questionable, it never fails to give an extravagant premium, in one shape or another, [whenever it borrows].[9]

Reputation—the reason your favorite restaurant keeps the bathroom clean—is a powerful motivator for governments that want to borrow. Indeed, one important, if still controversial, idea in economic history is that Britain's Glorious Revolution—when Catholic-sympathetic James II fled the country and was replaced by the Protestants King William and Queen Mary—was in large part a commitment of the state to make it clear that the lending class—the global pool of money of the seventeenth century—would always be repaid. Often billed as the rise of truly constitutional monarchy in Great Britain, with a monarch subject to the rule of law and hence subject to Parliament, the Glorious Revolution was in the eyes of many economic historians closer to a subjugation of king and Parliament to the lenders.

Before the Glorious Revolution, the idea that a monarch *must* repay lenders was considered absurd. How could a queen or king be at the beck and call of mere lenders of coin? But this power to repudiate loans meant that lenders were afraid to lend to monarchs, which in turn meant higher interest rates when monarchs really needed to borrow. The power to borrow at low interest rates relied on the commitment to repay, and the commitment to repay relied on a monarch strong enough to repay but weak enough to be forbidden from abjuring repayment.

The Glorious Revolution achieved this happy-enough medium, according to Nobelist Douglass North and Stanford political scientist Barry Weingast in an important essay.[10] By sacrificing power now— the power to repudiate sovereign debt—the government gained a reserve of potential power—the power to borrow on good terms when necessary. While there's still debate over how much this really explains the events of the Glorious Revolution, the political and economic logic is too strong to ignore.

The Powerlessness of Total Power

My George Mason University colleague Hilton Root has made a similar case for the French monarchy. In "Tying the King's Hands," Root argues that some of the cumbersome organizations of pre-Revolutionary France, often lumped together with the umbrella term of *corporations*, were in fact ways to make it socially and politically acceptable for French monarchs to credibly commit to repaying the money they borrowed. Root notes that

> during the Old Regime the main obstacle to efficient state finance was that the principal player—the king—was above the law. This meant that he could not be compelled to honor his debts and often chose to repudiate them. . . . The king paid a higher rate of interest than his wealthiest subjects due to his reputation for reneging on his debts.[11]

How could the king change this? Here we see the weakness of the cliché that political power grows out of the barrel of a gun. Instead, in times of financial trouble, political power grows out of a strong credit rating. And the way for the king to raise his credit rating was to find a credible way to give up a key part of his political power: the power to default.

Root describes one important way that kings of Old Regime France substantially surrendered this power: by borrowing from their nobles. A classic method of royal borrowing was for the king to sell a government job that would in turn have big payoffs to whoever bought the job; in particular, it might provide tax-free status for life. But it was risky to pay for such *secrétaire du roi* jobs: after a few years, the king might decide to fire you, make you start paying taxes again, and sell the job to somebody else. Once the king had a reputation for turning these jobs-for-life into jobs-at-will, people weren't willing to pay that much for them. The king's prerogative to change his mind became a weakness, not a strength.

The solution was for les secrétaires du roi to join together and form a mutual fund. They didn't call it that, but that's what it was. They called it a corporation instead. This corporation borrowed money from the public and used the proceeds to buy jobs for would-be secrétaires du roi; the investors in the corporation were repaid by the grateful secrétaires du roi over time, so the corporation paid de facto dividends. But if an individual secrétaire was fired by the king, the secrétaire no longer had to keep making payments. Firings were therefore bad news for the investors. When the king fired a noble in order to resell the office, he didn't just anger one noble; he angered and stirred distrust among all the investors in the corporation. Perhaps unsurprisingly, when faced with the prospect of hurting his reputation so publicly and with the prospect of damaging so many investors and palace insiders at once, the king behaved, well, less kingly, and more like a typical borrower, grudgingly keeping the promises of his past.

By borrowing money from a visible, public, widely owned pool of money, the kings of Old Regime France found a way to tie their own hands, and that made it easier to borrow at better rates. These kings voluntarily—not gladly, but voluntarily—surrendered their current power to default in order to increase their future power to borrow. The examples of both France and of Britain remind us that it's wise for governments, whether monarchies or democracies, to humble themselves before the mighty power of the lender.

Repaying Half the Debts of the Past to Increase the Loans of the Future

One way that governments humble themselves before lenders is by repaying most of what they owe even when times turn grim. As Sebastian Edwards of UCLA's business school reports, the typical nation that defaults on its debt the normal way—by telling bondholders, "We aren't going to repay the amounts we promised, when we promised"—still ends up paying about two-thirds of what they owe on average. The median defaulting country in his sample forced investors to take a 32% haircut, and because of a few extreme cases, the mean haircut was a little larger, 37%. Either way, the typical defaulting country repays most of the money.[12] Why does a defaulting government do this? Largely because it doesn't want to entirely ruin its reputation as a nation that pays its debts.

Like many other economists, I've joked that the United States should wait until the last baby boomer has cashed her last Social Security check and then entirely default on the national debt. Such a well-timed default would save the United States trillions of dollars in interest payments. But that won't happen for the same reason rich nations don't routinely default after racking up a big war debt: mostly because the government wants to be able to borrow again in the relatively near future. The most immediate, short-run reason governments need to borrow is simply to manage irregular cash flows over the course of the year. Just as retail businesses have to borrow from banks in the fall in order to fill the store shelves for the Christmas shopping season, governments need to take short-term loans to tide themselves over until taxes are due. And since governments in the rich democracies are mostly welfare states with a small bureaucracy attached, retirement checks and nurses' salaries need to be paid out every month or else the nation's social structure will collapse.

And even aside from the immediate month-to-month cash flow problems, governments want to be able to borrow for construction projects and other infrastructure investments. Furthermore, if worker productivity continues to increase at a rate of 1% or so per year, it makes good economic sense to borrow against some of the nation's future income every year, to live a little better now and repay that debt when you're richer a few decades from now. After all, if your nation will be earning 50% more per person in five decades, why not use the power of the global financial markets to pull some of the prosperity forward in time? Just as youth is wasted on the young, so is income wasted on the old. We can't do much about the former, but financial markets can help the younger me enjoy some the wealth that the older me will someday receive.

All of these factors—the need for fast cash, the need to fund capital projects, and the wisdom of smoothing out your lifetime consumer spending—mean that a nation that defaults will want to build a good reputation with the people who might lend to it in the future. And in practice, a key part of building that reputation is repaying as much of your debt as you can, especially when it hurts. The more that a defaulting government's austerity makes its citizens suffer and complain, the clearer it becomes that the government really is willing to go the extra mile to repay the lenders. The fact that the government is willing to endure today's citizen complaints in order to repay its loans sends a signal that the government might be reasonably reliable about repaying in the future. If instead the government were cavalier about defaulting today after a few anti-austerity whimpers on social media and couple of halfhearted protests about spending cutbacks, lenders would presume that the government would be relatively cavalier about defaulting in the future.

That means that present suffering amid a default is important to improving the government's future fiscal health—and it means that the present and future bondholders are already powerfully shaping government policy. Government policy today is shaped by bond-holder sentiment today. Since bondholders are already wielding this indirect but clear influence over government policy, we should con-sider formalizing that role.

A Brief History of Sovereign Default

Europeans saw the political power of bondholders in recent years in Greece, where in the aftermath of the European debt crisis, individual investors, banks, and international lending agencies placed strong pressure on the Greek government to curb spend-ing, increase taxes, and sell off government assets in order to create enough free cash flow to start repaying the Greek government's massive debts. Lenders became reformers.

Sovereign bondholders similarly became de facto reformers during the 1997 Asian financial crisis and even earlier in the 1980s during the Latin American debt crisis. The pattern is now almost routine: a finan-cial crisis hits, the economy weakens, and governments instantly lose tax revenue because people cut back on spending (fewer sales taxes) and people get laid off (fewer income taxes). At the same time, citizens have greater demands for extra spending through welfare programs, unemployment insurance, and job creation programs. Government ac-counting isn't all that different from your personal financial accounting. If your revenues are falling and your costs are going up, you're going to have a tough time making your monthly mortgage payment. Old financial commitments—to lenders in particular—that were easy to meet in good times become tougher to meet in bad times.

In the most famous cases, international agencies enter the story at this point—the International Monetary Fund (IMF), perhaps the World Bank or one of the regional development banks like the Inter-American Development Bank or the Asian Development Bank. In both the popular imagination and to some degree in reality, they're the harsh taskmasters of the global financial system. They're the ones that tell a developing country that it needs to eat its spinach before it can get dessert. These agencies offer to lend the crisis-suffering government enough to make it through the rough patch, often including enough to pay off debts coming due. But in return, the international agencies demand reforms that they believe will help the government to repay these loans in the future.

In real life, banks do this all the time. If you borrow money to buy a house, the bank insists on seeing proof of your homeowner's insurance, for instance. If your house burns down and it is uninsured, and you decide to walk away from the mortgage, the bank will wind up with some land and a charred husk of a home. Since it doesn't want to end up in that position, the mortgage comes with a string attached: the requirement of homeowner's insurance.

Business lending comes with even more strings. Banks reserve the right to see a business's books, as well as to check the business's inventory to make sure that the business owner hasn't squirreled the bank's money away in an overseas account. Accountants do much of this checking on the bank's behalf. An accountant I know had to personally climb to the top of a grain silo in the American Midwest as part of a regular audit; she climbed up a silo half a dozen stories high just to peer into the top of the silo and make sure that it really was filled with grain. Insisting on specific actions, following up, verifying the claims of borrowers: this is a natural part of the business of lending.

But when it comes to sovereign lending, there's an unusual split. While crisis lenders like the IMF or the World Bank insist on reform as a condition for loans, the everyday lenders—those who buy government bonds during good times—play a much more passive role. In pleasant times, international investors—mutual funds, investment banks, insurance companies—calmly take a look at a government's credit rating, read some newspapers and perhaps check out some statistical analyses, and decide whether the return on the government's sovereign bonds is worth the risk of default.

Defining a New Relationship

These arm's-length relationships are absurdly inefficient. Instead, the role of sovereign bondholders should be redefined to become more like that of a corporate shareholder. By thinking of sovereign bondholders as sovereign shareholders, the types of reforms I've suggested will appear natural and evolutionary rather than radical— not 50% less democracy but closer to 10%. Recall that in the private sector, there are two classic ways for a business to raise funds:

1. Borrowing, through banks or by issuing bonds: Someone gives me money now and I promise to repay that amount plus interest later

2. Issuing equity or "shares of stock" or "partial ownership": Someone gives me money now and I promise to let her have some share of future profits (to be determined later!) plus a voice in how to run the business.

There are lots of exceptions, but those are the two big divides. Bonds mean a promise of money but no voice, and shares mean a voice but only the vaguest promises of money.

There's one big exception: if you're a bondholder and the company can't repay you, the company goes bankrupt. But bankruptcy needn't mean that the company shuts down immediately, closing the doors and selling the furniture to pay off the outstanding bills. For big companies, bankruptcy rarely means a complete shutdown. Instead, bankruptcy typically means—in both law and the real world—that the bondholders now get their own shot at running the company. In a conventional private sector setting, bondholders are potential future shareholders. I'm suggesting that in the rich democracies, where the closest thing we have to government "shareholders" are the voting citizens, we blur the line between bondholders and voters. We should start to think of bondholders as democracy's high-level financial councilors, advisers with real skin in the game.

Outsourcing the Toughest Choices to Bondholders

In the mid-1990s, amid growing awareness that governments had to respond to the demands of potential investors, columnist Thomas Friedman wrote a column on the growing political force of sovereign bondholders and the rating agencies. I quoted from it earlier; here he goes on to illustrate how bond markets help improve governance: "Moody's and the bond market are now imposing on democracies economic and political decisions that the democracies, left to their own devices, simply cannot take."[13] The national debt may be one of the best checks on short-run voter thinking, but even so, the distant voice of the bond markets has yet to stir most rich democracies to embrace fiscal sustainability.

Over the next few decades, partly because of an aging populace and partly because of slower growth, government debts are likely to increase as a percentage of the typical rich democracy's national income. The ratio of government debt to national income is now around 200% in Japan, the rich nation with the oldest population. Many other rich nations are already over 100%; Italy is over 150%. For six of the seven G-7 countries (Canada the welcome exception), these ratios are higher than in the mid-1990s, when the Man from Moody's was calling for fiscal discipline. With government debt levels expected to remain so high for so long, foreshadowing an era of difficult financial choices, the political implications are obvious: reducing the power of voters by increasing the power of the crucial lending class is an idea who time is already here.

7 Jonathan Rauch, Prophet of Political Realism

> In order for governments to govern, political machines or
> something like them need to exist, and they need to work.
> **JONATHAN RAUCH**

GEORGE WASHINGTON PLUNKITT told the people how democracy really
worked. And crucially, this Napoleon of corruption demonstrated
how to make democracy work better. Plunkitt was a leader in New
York City's Tammany Hall—a Democratic Party political club that in
the late 1800s and early 1900s dominated New York City's politics.
But how did the Tammany machine work? According to Plunkitt,
mostly through what he called "honest graft": by making money off
insider deals—off what you knew and whom you knew, not by steal-
ing the government's tax revenue.[1] In *Plunkitt of Tammany Hall: A
Series of Very Plain Talks on Very Practical Politics,* Plunkitt told his
tales to Gilded Age journalist William Riordan, and the short book
has become a staple of courses on American politics ever since.

Plunkitt wasn't a crook; instead, as he put it, "He seen his opportunities and he took 'em."[2] But how did he get those opportunities? And how did the Tammany machine stay in power for so long?
Let's start with the very definition of staying in power—getting
reelected—and build from there. Plunkitt gave sound advice on how
to get reelected and offered personal examples:

> For instance, here's how I gather in the young men. I hear of a
> young feller that's proud of his voice, thinks that he can sing fine.

> I ask him to come around to Washington Hall and join our Glee
> Club. He comes and sings, and he's a follower of Plunkitt for life.
> Another young feller gains a reputation as a baseball player in a
> vacant lot. I bring him into our baseball club. That fixes him. You'll
> find him workin' for my ticket at the polls next election day.[3]

Plunkitt reminds us that as Carol Hanisch wrote in 1970, the personal is political.[4] Plunkitt describes his take on that approach: "I don't trouble them with political arguments. I just study human nature and act accordin'."[5]

Plunkitt built up a network of loyal followers, but loyalty to Plunkitt didn't require Churchill's blood, toil, tears, and sweat; it typically just required grabbing a few of your friends to vote the Tammany ticket on election day. That's what it takes to build a powerful political machine: a network of people who'll show up to vote for your cause when it counts.

The Power of Transactional Politics

Just because a team is loyal to its leader doesn't mean the team will use its powers for good; evil political parties and murderous organizations are common throughout history. At the least, though, strong, cooperative teams are a prerequisite for large-scale social improvement. Let's return to the example of the U.S. Congress. I earlier described it as a reelection factory, a system designed by the visible hand of politicians so that members of Congress can show the good people back home that their members are doing something valuable for them. It's a machine designed for credible credit claiming.

But Congress is something else besides a reelection factory. When talking among friends, I don't describe Congress as a reelection factory; I use another old metaphor for Congress: a favor factory. Members do favors for voters back home in exchange for political support—but they also do favors for other members, including members of the congressional leadership; and they do favors for the president, supporting a bill they might not particularly like. They do those favors not out of the kindness of their heart or because it's for the good of the country—at least not as a rule. Instead, these favors are all part of the norm of reciprocity, what the experts call reciprocal altruism: you scratch my back, and I'll scratch yours.

That's a key ingredient for getting things done in Washington. When it shows up in the form of votes for a piece of legislation, it's known as logrolling: "I'm not crazy about your bill, but if you throw in a sweetener [a real political term] that helps out the voters back in my district, I can bring myself to vote 'Aye.'" Logrolling apparently refers to "a former American custom of neighbors assisting one another in rolling logs into a pile for burning,"[6] but now, as the Merriam-Webster's dictionary notes, it can refer to any exchange of favors. In practice, it's most often used in the field of politics, and it refers to cutting deals when trying to pass legislation, not through threats but through legislative favors. It's "an Aye for an Aye."

Democracy Needs Corruption to Succeed

Donald Wittman, an economist at the University of California at Santa Cruz, wrote an excellent book, *The Myth of Democratic Failure*, that has shaped my thinking about democracy, particularly about the promise and potential of democracy.[7] Wittman argues that democracies are in a good position to help the economy grow and to give voters largely what they want, in part because of the power of logrolling.

To illustrate: if 40% of members of the U.S. House of Representatives really want a piece of legislation, and they want it badly enough, then they'll willingly include some targeted tax breaks, health care spending expansions, or changes in airline regulations so they can get another 12% to 15% of members to vote for the bill. Start with the voters you have and build your coalition from there, one favor at a time . . . Plunkitt himself couldn't have done any better. There are endless issues where small- to medium-sized groups of legislators care a lot about an issue, and the way to get the legislature—indeed, the nation—to do something about the issue is with some logrolling.

Logrolling would be impossible in a pure democracy, with everyone voting on their smartphones to consider this or that bill; it would be fruitless to try to cut a deal across millions of citizens. But put a hundred—or maybe a few hundred—elected officials into a legislature? That just might work. Indeed, that's just how it does work. As Wittman put it in a related academic article, "The small number of members in the House and Senate reduces negotiation costs, thereby creating the conditions for efficient logrolling."[8]

One way to make a logroll work is with earmarks—targeted spending that helps a particular member of Congress. Rather than saying, "The Department of the Transportation shall fund such bridge projects as its experts see fit," a piece of legislation might rephrase things slightly, to "shall fund a five-lane bridge in Schenectady, New York." Earmarks are often the glue that makes the logroll stick.

Earmarks are so important that when the U.S. Congress formally banned the practice in early 2010, I predicted that the ban would make it tougher, not easier, for Congress to be fiscally prudent. In January 2010, a year before the GOP retook the House, I tweeted, "The key to controlling spending is permitting more earmarks (*sic*)."[9]

After all, my thinking went, each individual member of Congress (particularly on the Republican side) might wish for low spending for everyone else, but each individual member also wants more spending for her own district. The practical way to cement a spending cut deal would be to hand out a few dozen well-targeted earmarks to the most pro-spending members of Congress in exchange for a pro-spending-cut vote. (Even if the earmarks add up, they won't add up to much; at their peak, earmarks were no more than 1% of total U.S. federal spending.[10]) We'll all hold hands and jump into the void, even if some of us have to be paid to hold hands.

When the Republicans retook the House in 2011, the GOP stuck to the no-earmark promise on paper, and more or less in practice. At that point, House GOP members, fueled by Tea Party ideas of fiscal prudence, were verbally and to some degree personally committed to cutting back the growth rate of spending. In 2011 and for a while later, there was no particular pressure for tax cuts, and the GOP had just picked up sixty-three seats in the House of Representatives, yielding its largest majority in decades. By normal political measures, the GOP was in a good position to pass the spending bills that it wanted, even though it faced a Senate and a presidency controlled by the Democratic party. So how did my prediction turn out?

For a couple of years, I was wildly incorrect. With the Senate held by Democrats and the House held by Republicans, it became obvious that the real deal to cut wasn't within the House, but between the House and the Senate. If the upper and lower bodies of the legislature couldn't work together, nothing was going to happen. And amazingly, the two bodies worked together and enacted what for the time counted as fiscal austerity: substantial reductions in spending compared to the old plans. The details I'll skip—it included the "sequester"—but it meant the House was able to impose much of its will on national legislation without earmarks. My theory didn't hold up too well at the time.

But I'm a scholar who focuses on the long run, on the underlying social mechanisms. I enjoy a good anecdote, an exception to a rule, but I was convinced that cooperation, collaboration, and team building were central to passing legislation in any broadly democratic political system; that Plunkitt's wisdom was real; and that most of the time in politics, give-and-take matters more than lofty ideals. I was willing to bide my time.

And I think time has treated my claim fairly well. In the U.S. Congress, with the decline of earmarks, the biggest games left in town are ideological outrage, social media grandstanding, and other behaviors that make individual politicians more willing to stand up to party leaders. Earmarks and other targeted goodies that the late University of Maryland economist Mancur Olson called "selective benefits" are important for cutting everyday political deals—for giving politicians something to work for beyond another viral appearance on social media. My colleague Tyler Cowen and I have discussed earmarks off and on since 2010; he wrote a column in 2018 on the still-underappreciated merits of earmarks. Here's what he had to say: "Most of all, I think of earmarks as recognizing that compromise and messiness are bound to remain essential features of American government, and that, whether we like it or not, there is something inherently *transactional* [emphasis added] about being governed."[11]

And in order to stick, these transactions need some distance from the voters.

Political Machines: A Tool for Focusing on the Future

This brings us to Jonathan Rauch: journalist, pundit, and, dare I say, scholar. Rauch is the real deal, having written multiple books on social science topics that have had broad influence both inside and outside academia. Also, he's fantastic in person; I've met him socially a couple of times. If you get a chance to talk with him about any of the topics he's written about—including happiness research, the battle for marriage equality, treating your introverted loved ones well, sluggish governance, and political correctness—you're in for a real treat.

In 2015, he published a short, excellent book that he made freely available: *Political Realism: How Hacks, Machines, Big Money, and Back-Room Deals Can Strengthen American Democracy*. He defines his term at length:

> What, then, is political realism? . . . It sees governing as difficult and political peace and stability as treasures never to be taken for granted. It understands that power's complex hydraulics make interventions unpredictable and risky. (Banning some ugly political practice, for instance, won't necessarily make it go away.) . . . Back-scratching and logrolling are signs of a healthy political system, not a corrupt one. *Transactional* [emphasis added] politics is not always appropriate or effective, but a political system which is not reliably capable of it is a system in a state of critical failure.[12]

You'll see that I italicized the word *transactional* both here and in Tyler Cowen's quote above. Both scholars think that real-world political success depends on insiders cutting deals, deals that outsiders—regular voters like you and me—might be appalled by. Rauch offers one particular reason why transactional politics tends to enlarge the pie: because often, the political machine—which might include both a formal party apparatus as well as an informal back-scratching operation that spans the world of lobbying, campaign donations, and legislation—has an interest in the long run. The machine has a longer political life than most politicians, so it cares whether the country will be rich enough, stable enough, safe enough, for it to remain strong for decades to come. The machine has patience, a trait lacking in politics, as Rauch notes: "Politicians, like voters, are short-sighted, and machines help with that, too, because they [the machines] are capable of strategizing and transacting across time. Machines are to politics as banking is to the economy: being long-term, repeat players, they can extend something like political credit."[13] A longer time horizon is just what democracies need, and machines are a critical tool for extending that horizon.

True in Theory

But even if we agree with Wittman and Cowen and Rauch, is transactional politics truly less democratic? If the U.S. Congress moved 10% in the direction of Tammany, would that be democracy reducing? Rauch suggests that the answer is yes, at least "to some extent": "An 'insulated' system [one with a powerful machine] is *to some extent undemocratic* [emphasis added] . . . yet it can also provide leaders with the critical margin of support that they need when difficult policy choices have to be made."[14]

And politics in the rich democracies will continue to be a realm of "difficult policy choices." Between Rauch's push for backroom deals and Blinder's push for a national tax board, one might suggest, jocularly, that these two excellent, influential Brookings Institution scholars appear to be pushing for a grand total of 4% less democracy. A fine start.

Mandatory Discussion of the Perils of Social Media

> What the country faces is not a crisis of leadership but a crisis of followership.
>
> Jonathan Rauch

Rauch's quote illustrates the plight of the modern Congress, but it also illustrates the power of social media to fragment national cultures. Martin Gurri, a former CIA analyst and a careful observer of global events, makes the latter point in his recent book, *The Revolt of the Public and the Crisis of Authority in the New Millennium*. Gurri started off as an old-school foreign policy analyst, and over the decades he has watched the changes wrought by the rise of television, blogs, and now full-blown social media on the worlds of technology and politics the world over. Gurri describes how things used to work, in days of "old long since," *auld lang syne*: "As an analyst of global events, my source material came from parsing the world's newspapers and television reports. That was what I considered information."[15]

That's of course no longer the way of the world. Now, newspapers and TV are just two ingredients, no longer even critical ingredients, in the global information stew.

One of Gurri's illustrations comes from looking at the dog that didn't bark, the story that didn't get covered. As is well known, the Arab Spring found its catalyst—Gurri's tragically descriptive word—in a photo posted on Facebook of Mohamed Bouazizi, a Tunisian street vendor who set himself on fire amid deep despair after enduring humiliations from government officials. This one man's sacrifice set off a regional revolution; Bouazizi was posthumously awarded the European Union's prestigious Sakharov Prize for Freedom of Thought, a sign of his importance in spurring the Arab Spring. But Gurri draws our attention to another Tunisian street vendor, Abdesslem Trimech, who also set himself on fire after his own set of humiliations at the hands of government officials. Like Bouazizi,

Trimech died from his wounds—nine months before Bouazizi made the same sacrifice. Bouazizi's death, the one shared on Facebook, created a revolution. Trimech's offline death did not.

And this power, the power of bottom-up stories spread online to break into global consciousness and change the world around us, grows stronger by the year. Gurri's examples are wide-ranging, from Napster heralding the rise of widespread music (and now movie and book) file sharing, to Turkish President Erdoğan's rage against Twitter posts. Together, they illustrate how the power of media gatekeepers has plummeted in the information age. This weakening power of cultural gatekeepers leads to Gurri's "crisis of public authority." In modern democracies, there's no authoritative Walter Cronkite; in autocracies, it's at least possible, and now often easy, to mock the autocrat, to share information he doesn't want shared, to find—well, if not the truth, then at least an alternative story line.

In the United States in particular, citizens and elites alike have worried that in this new information ecosystem, it has become easier for rogue actors—like Chinese and Russian intelligence—to create viral messages that can shift political debates, exacerbate political tensions, or both. And that's a major, legitimate concern. But it is also just one consequence among many of Gurri's crises of public authority. A world of ill-informed voters who have a strong desire to filter reality through their chosen lenses is close to a world where Keynes's law is true: demand creates its own supply. If people want to see certain types of news stories—perhaps where my team is suffering unjustly and the other team isn't playing fair—then an invisible hand, an act of entrepreneurship, will create such news stories. And when the invisible hand creates—or just reframes—news events, it never *feels* like fake news; it feels like a truth deeper than mere news, better than mere history. As the Batman says at the end of Christopher Nolan's *The Dark Knight*, "Sometimes the truth isn't good enough. Sometimes people deserve more."[16]

All too often, citizens of rich democracies enter that world of better-than-truth. Different subcultures across these nations hear different narratives, each narrative meeting a demand for a custom-made truth. What does this new realm of decentralized, entrepreneurial, cocooned media bubbles mean for good government? Perhaps it means that voter ignorance will rise, strengthening the argument for moderate epistocracy. It's too early to say whether that's the case; further research truly is needed. But there's one likely effect of declining public authority that I foresee, and it has a clear implication for good government:

> If the rise of social media–driven politics means that cultural fads or even orchestrated outside influences are creating bigger short-term shocks to the national political debate (a big if!), then any given election will be doing a worse job than it used to of taking the "national political temperature."

In other words, if there's more noise in the public sphere, then any one election tells us less about what the public is really saying. If one goal of an election is to find out what the people really want—and that's certainly a good, if incomplete, goal for electoral democracy—then we probably want to measure the public's enduring interests and wishes, not a random swing to the left or right occurring a week before an election. And the bigger the random swings, the stronger the argument is for not listening too closely to any one election.

Statisticians understand the principle at work here: when your data grow noisier, you should pay less attention to any particular piece of data and instead should look at a bigger sample before drawing any conclusions. If a song is playing in a noisy room, you'll need to listen to more of it to make sure that it really is the Rolling Stones's profound reflection on the problem of evil, "Sympathy for the Devil."

What's the solution to a related problem, the problem of noisy elections? Here's one possibility: staggered elections, so that each election has a lower stake. The U.S. Senate already does this, but it could have been otherwise. With the Senate's six-year terms, it would in principle be easy to have all one hundred senators up for reelection in 2020, then all one hundred again in 2026 and 2032.

Fortunately, that's not the way the U.S. Constitution set things up. Instead, one-third of all senators are up for reelection every two years—slowing turnover, making the Senate's personification of the body politic more emotionally and intellectual stable from year to year. Any country with four, six, or (a professor can dream!) eight-year terms could easily stagger out the terms to create what the Senate calls "a continuing body." And one benefit of a continuing body is that it will have a more stable, more coherent mind.

Finding paths to good democratic governance amid Gurri's crisis of public authority will take more than our modern varieties of secular preaching: it will take more than just clever tweets and memorable newspaper columns that stick up for evidence-based news and dispassionate analysis. Instead, the rich democracies will need institutional changes to dampen the effects of news shocks and increase the weight of the better informed. Staggered elections aren't the only tool for improving governance in today's truthiness-driven democracies, but they're a good first step. Here's to hoping we find a full staircase of such good steps.

8 The Hard Case of the European Union

Europe is worse than anything because there isn't even
the parody of representative democracy. It's a pure
oligarchy, Europe.

MICHEL HOUELLEBECQ

IF THERE'S A WORLD-RECOGNIZED ICON of wasteful, out-of -touch, elitist bureaucrats telling people what to do, it's the European Union (EU). Surveys repeatedly show that when you ask Europeans who live in EU countries what they think about their supranational government, complaints about a wasteful, out-of-touch bureaucracy are common—and even if the complaints aren't a roar, they're at least a solid rumble. For over a decade, the Eurobarometer survey, run by the EU itself, repeatedly asked thousands of EU citizens this question: "What does the European Union mean to you personally?"

Respondents could choose from a list of about a dozen possible answers, and they could choose as many as they thought were a good fit. It was a balanced menu of possible responses, with the same number of positives (like social protection and economic prosperity) and negatives (crime, loss of border control). An EU report that looked back on survey results from 2002 to 2015 noted that the fourth and fifth most popular responses tended to be "bureaucracy" and "waste of money" year in and year out. And each of these terms tended to come up in at least 20% of survey responses. The same EU report noted that those two responses "have been gradually increasing [in popularity] since 2002."[1]

So if it's a good idea to dial down democracy just a tad, then why do so many people complain about the EU? Is it mostly because of out-of-touch oligarchs at the EU's headquarters in Brussels, as Houellebecq's quote implies? Or is it instead mostly the democratic elements of the EU—the elected officials themselves—that are the bigger source of trouble? I contend that it's mostly the latter. When the EU bureaucracy is handed a task by the EU's democratically elected leaders, the bureaucracy does an at least competent and often impressive job by the standards of real-world governments. The problems the EU has struggled with most intensely during the past few decades—as it became, in fits and starts, not just a customs union originally known as the European Coal and Steel Community but a full-fledged government with a central bank, a functioning judiciary, and a vast regulatory apparatus—are mostly problems of democratic governance, not of oligarchic governance. If the voters had insisted on steering the Brussels bus themselves—through regular referenda, an elected president of Europe, or elections for top EU regulators— things would probably have been worse.

The unique structure of the EU, driven by democratic realities and by the difficulties of coming to agreement when the continent's voters have such ideological diversity, certainly creates problems. But the structure is no mere accident, no mere mistake made by oligarchs during a planning session in the distant past. Instead, the complicated, difficult, nearly unmanageable structure of the EU is the natural result of trying to create a democracy with such a diverse set of over half a billion voters spread across dozens of different, largely sovereign nations, who together democratically choose the direction of the EU.

In short, Europe was a tough place to build a supranational democracy. It's impressive that they've done as well as they have.

The Democratic EU

The EU has three crucial governing bodies: the European Parliament, the Council of the European Union, and the European Commission. The first is democratically elected, the second, effectively so, and the third is led by people appointed by the council, confirmed by a European Parliament majority, and hold office for renewable five-year terms.

The European Parliament (EP) is in many ways a typical parliament; its elections are held every five years, simultaneously across all of Europe. Each nation gets a certain number of seats based heavily, but not entirely, on population; there's a thumb on the scales to give more seats to less populous countries. The EP uses a proportional representation system to decide how many seats in parliament are given to each political party. The general rule—skipping details and exceptions—is that the proportion of votes a party gets determines the proportion of seats that party gets. So very loosely, if your party gets 8% of the vote across the country, it will get 8% of the seats in the European Parliament, even if your party's voters are scattered across the country. That means that individual members of the EP don't represent small geographic districts the way that members of the British House of Commons or the U.S. Congress; instead, they typically represent some mix of their party and their entire country. This means that small political parties that would have a tough time winning an outright majority in a small congressional district or parliamentary constituency can still earn quite a few seats in the EP.

The Council of the European Union is in some ways the EU's version of a senate, a small upper body with substantial legislative power and some unwritten de facto executive power. It's fair to simplify by calling it a quasi-senate. The Council of the European Union is in some ways the EU's senate, a small upper body with substantial legislative power and some unwritten de facto executive power. The Council consists of government ministers—finance ministers, labor ministers, foreign ministers, and the like—who represent each of the twenty-eight member states of the EU. This EU Council has a twin, the European Council, made up of the prime ministers, presidents, and heads of government of the same twenty-eight member states. The EU Council legislates, while the European Council makes nominations to key EU positions. The EU council is where all twenty-eight EU member governments—themselves democratically elected—vote on key issues; and the biggest issues—like admitting new EU members, defining the rights of EU citizens, and rules for harmonizing national tax policy among EU members—typically require a unanimous vote. That means that frequently, a single EU nation can stop the legislative process. Pulling the EU's emergency brake like that is risky and reputationally costly to the nation that pulls it, but the fact that it's there makes each government a bit more comfortable handing power over to Brussels. And when decisions aren't made unanimously, they are most often made through a supermajority process, qualified majority voting. Simple majority voting is reserved for mundane matters or occasionally and controversially when it's clear a majority-backed proposal would fail under qualified majority or unanimity voting. The Council consists of a small group of powerful individuals—powerful as both agenda setters and voters.

Every piece of legislation has to pass both an EP vote and a Council vote. The first vote puts a lot of weight on countries with higher population (like the U.S. House of Representatives), and the second puts equal weight on every single country in the EU (like the U.S. Senate) unless—and in the EU there's typically an "unless"—the Council vote is one of the qualified majority votes. A qualified majority vote has elements of both equal country weight (at least 55% of nations have to approve) and equal population weight (countries representing at least 65% of EU citizens have to approve). The sixteen smallest countries, in other words, can't pass something through the Council by a qualified majority vote, though the smaller countries could in principle pass something through the Council if the vote required just a simple majority. Passing laws in the EU is no small matter. But the barriers to passage are democratic ones: majority votes and (often) unanimous agreement or (more often) supermajority agreement. This is nothing if not representative democracy.

The third crucial organ of EU governance is the European Commission (EC). The EC has all the conventional executive powers in the EU, though it has no authority over the European Central Bank, itself an independent creation of the EU. The EC supervises approximately 32,000 employees and contractors who implement policy that has been enacted by the EP and the Council. The EC itself has dozens of members—one key member from each EU nation and a lot of underlings.

The EC is led by a president, who, like its other members, is appointed by the twenty-eight European governments and approved by the EP. The president of the EC really is the president of Europe in an important sense, but not in the usual political sense of being the top boss. He or she is more like the president of a large corporation. In a corporation, the president handles the day-to-day decisions of the business, implementing the grand strategy set by the chief executive officer (CEO). Similarly, the EC president is less like a corporate CEO—setting grand strategy—and instead is largely implementing policies created by the real bosses—the EP and particularly the Council. There are exceptions of course—there are always exceptions—but that's the rule.

This captures the essence of European governance: divided power, some weight to countries with more population, but ultimately—since the Council frequently requires a supermajority or even a unanimous vote—the small states have enormous power to stop any legislation in its tracks. A reminder: the EC is the executive branch. Though it has sole power to propose legislation, its proposals can be and are frequently amended. Any laws that the EP and the EU Council agree to must be enforced by the European Commission.

The EU sounds a lot like a democracy, because by modern standards, it is.

The Illusory "Democratic Deficit"

The EU is voter shaped, but that's not the same as saying that it's a typical rich-country democratic government. The differences, however, are less on the "democracy" side and more on the "government" side. Yes, as every commentator on the EU notes, the EU has zero direct power to tax and instead lives on the contributions of member states. The long-term EU budget is subject to a unanimous vote of the Council, ensuring that every nation has a voice and raising the bargaining power of the poorest, least-populous states. Also, the EU as an organization has no military power of its own, and its police arm, Europol, has no power to arrest a person. So it's a government without some of the key features we take for granted: no power to tax and no military or police to directly enforce its wishes.

That means that most of the EU's power is in the "what remains" category: regulatory power. As Princeton's Andrew Moravcsik has noted in an excellent and widely discussed essay on whether the EU's democracy is legitimate, that means the EU focuses on the just the issues that most governments leave to independent agencies or to other branches of government that in most democracies are far from the media spotlight.[2] If you're interested in the moral concept of democratic legitimacy, Moravcsik's argument is relevant: he's here to remind us that *if* the EU had little democracy, *then* it would still be a reasonable form of governance because it's mostly sticking to tasks that fans of democracy typically leave to unelected bureaucrats. But let's remember something else: the EU is still quite democratic by conventional standards. So any complaints that scholars or citizens or pundits care to lodge about it aren't really complaints about technocracy or oligarchy or the so-called democratic deficit in Brussels, at least compared to other real-world democracies. There are plenty of elections, the European Parliament as a whole has a lot of power, the entirely elected Council has even more power, and as political researchers Morten Egeberg, Åse Gornitzka, and Jarle Trondal of the University of Oslo conclusively document, officials from the EC meet frequently, both formally and informally, with members of the European Parliament, providing information and listening to them.[3] There's little doubt that members of the Brussels bureaucracy respond to phone calls from leading EU politicians and pay close attention to their de jure and de facto bosses. By conventional standards, the EU acts like a responsive democratic government. That means that the core remaining question is not whether the EU is democratic but whether it's working.

10% Less Democracy: The Brussels Case Study

Since the EU acts like a modern democracy, that means it has elements of nondemocracy, of powerful, fairly autonomous bureaucrats, as in the European Court of Justice, the EC's regulatory agencies, and beyond. The case for the EU as quasi-oligarchy (to adapt Houellebecq's term) is even stronger for the European Central Bank (ECB), created in 1999 and overseeing the economic fortunes of the eurozone, the nineteen EU countries that use the euro. The members of the ECB's executive board and the president of the Bank itself are chosen by the twenty-eight European Governments and hold eight-year terms. And as noted, members of the European Parliament serve five-year terms.

So while the EU is substantially democratic, it has important less democratic elements. Taken together, this means that the EU ought to serve as an excellent example of many of the democracy-reducing reforms I've suggested throughout this book. The EU has:

- Elected officials with reasonably long terms (Chapter 2)

- An extremely "independent" (that is, undemocratic) central bank (Chapter 3)

- Abundant "independent" regulatory agencies (and a fairly powerful and autonomous European Court of Justice) (Chapter 4)

- A relatively well-informed electorate, since the educated are disproportionately likely to vote in EP elections[4] (Chapter 5)

If the claims of earlier chapters are correct, then it's not too much to expect some good performance from the EU. Maybe not perfection— that's never the real-world standard—but at least some signs that a more detached, more oligarchical form of government yields real benefits without creating even bigger costs.

Here's some evidence: The EU is actually pretty popular overall. A 2018 survey of citizens across the EU reports typical results: "67 percent [of EU citizens] believe their country has benefited from EU membership, according to the survey, and 60 percent say being part of the bloc remains a good thing. (12 percent say it's bad for their country.)"[5]

The ECB has delivered low, stable inflation since its creation—far lower than the average inflation rate that southern Europe had had in previous decades, and even lower than Germany's post–World War II inflation rate. The ECB responded to the global financial crisis aggressively and creatively—even generating negative interest rates, charging banks that stored money at the European Central Bank rather than lending it out. And when the ECB was faced with massive debt problems in a few member states—debt that was created by quite democratic governments, by the way—it took aggressive and risky bets by buying up substantial amounts of the government debt of Italy, Spain, and others on the European periphery in a bid to preserve European harmony. Fingers crossed, but so far, so good.

And while the EU may get bad press for making it illegal to put little unmarked bottles of olive oil on your restaurant table,[6] it's reasonable to believe that joining the EU helps your nation's economy perform better overall. Economist Robert Lawson of Southern Methodist University and, separately, economist Andrew Young of Texas Tech University both coauthored studies finding that nations that join the EU increase their levels of economic freedom just a little more than other comparable countries.[7] These economic freedom indexes are widely used proxies for being market oriented, and since being market oriented rather than *dirigiste* is a good predictor of long-run prosperity, then the olive oil anecdotes are more the widely retweeted exception than the boring everyday rule. On average, joining the EU likely makes a nation more prosperous.

Part of the reason for this apparent effect of EU membership on pro-market orientation is that as part of the process of preparing to join the EU, nations have to present evidence that they have their act reasonably together. They have to show that they're reasonably democratic, have relatively market-oriented policies, and have governments that are competent by European standards. As Hungary's recent push for "illiberal democracy" demonstrates, past performance is no guarantee of future results. EU members can backslide after they get adopted into the family, and it's always hard to decide whether to punish or even evict a family member after making bad life choices. But the big push that national governments make when they want to join the EU probably works a lot like the news that you've just been hired to be the star of an action film: it's excellent motivation to get in shape.

Taken together, there's reasonable evidence that the EU delivers the goods. There are certainly bad reasons a nation might want to join the EU—to get in line for those luxurious EU agricultural sector subsidies, for instance—but there seems to have been an invisible (or is it visible?) hand at work in the process of EU accession. It's a club that's typically well worth joining, partly because the other club members nudge you to work out just a little bit harder. The nudges are irritating, but irritation is the price of motivation.

The Unsurprising Case of Brexit

If the club is so good, why would anyone want to leave? Does the Brexit vote—the referendum passed in 2016 by a slim majority of U.K. voters demanding to leave the EU—count as strong evidence against the EU's merits? Not at all. Remember, the EU is in part a pro-market club. It started as a club pushing for freer trade among European states, after all. At the same time, it is also heavily democratic, so it can push only for policies that receive wide support among the club members. The average member of the club has a big influence on the club's policies—and that fact shapes the question of how much the United Kingdom can benefit from EU membership.

Typically, when joining any organization where the other members will have an influence on you—where peer effects are real—you don't want to be one of the top performers in the organization. You want a lot of members who are better than you:

- Fellow gym members who can inspire you

- Fellow classmates who are smarter than you and can therefore teach you new things

- Fellow heads of government in the Council of Europe who are more market oriented than you

When our peers shape us, it's smart to search out peers who are better than us.

And in the EU, there aren't that many nations that can serve as models to the United Kingdom. Great Britain, after all, largely invented the concept of market-oriented liberalism, building on the insights of Adam Smith's late eighteenth-century work, *The Wealth of Nations*, and turning market-oriented liberalism into a practical policy that reached its peak in the late nineteenth century under the political leadership of Prime Minister William Gladstone. And while the United Kingdom has ebbed and flowed in its support for economic liberalism in the twentieth and twenty-first centuries, it still is far more market oriented than most other EU members.

Consider two standard indicators of economic liberalism, measures of a broadly more market-oriented economy: the Fraser Institute's Economic Freedom of the World and the Heritage Foundation's Index of Economic Freedom. Compared to other EU members, the former index rates only Ireland and Estonia higher than the United Kingdom, while the Index of Economic Freedom adds Denmark. That makes for just three nations out of twenty-eight EU members that follow Adam Smith's advice more than the United Kingdom does. Every time the British prime minister showed up at an EU summit, she was representing just about the most economically liberal country in the room. She was one of the fittest people at the policy gym, the bright student who had little to learn from her weaker classmates.

Part of the reason to join the EU is that it acts like an outside consultant, a coach, someone who motivates you to bring out your best effort. But how much good advice can you get from a coach who never accomplished that much compared to you? There's a good case to be made that countries that have a tough time embracing market-leaning reforms can use EU membership to help commit to better economic policies. For them, the EU is a wise, experienced consultant, a coach who knows what it's like to create winners. But for the United Kingdom, the case for membership was always closer to the "meh" side: whatever the benefits of membership were for Poland and France and Spain, they were always going to be weaker for the United Kingdom.

Obviously the Brexit vote was motivated by much more than rules from Brussels about food labels, and immigration policy is at the top of the list of the concerns of UK voters. But UK voters and politicians alike can to some extent weigh the benefits of EU membership against the costs. And somewhere on the list of costs is the fact that the UK has better policies and better governance than the typical EU member. It's hard to prevent the fitter members of the gym from leaving—and in this case, for a variety of complex reasons, it looks like one of the fittest decided it was time to go.

Democracy amid Diversity: A Better Explanation for the EU's Problems

The EU's greatest struggles since the global financial crisis—to address the European debt crises, the migration crisis, and the rise of illiberal democracies in portions of Europe—are substantially caused by the EU's democratic structure. The EU, slow to come to a decision on each of these matters and then finding it impossible to enforce the so-called decision it announces, can't make up its mind because it consists of such diverse minds, each of which has strong, often overwhelming power to stop the governance process. Political scientists, sociologists, and economists have all found different forms of evidence that higher levels of cultural and ethnic diversity tend to generate political conflict and distrust, most famously in Robert Putnam's research on trust in one's neighbors.[8] Higher levels of cultural and ethnic diversity also appear to reduce cooperation and productivity—as shown in both a lab experiment at Harvard University[9] and a flower processing factory in Kenya.[10]

It's difficult for Europe's diverse collection of nations to come to an agreement, in part because it's difficult for any diverse political coalition to act in an organized manner, to act like an *organization*. An old American saying by the cowboy philosopher Will Rogers is relevant: "I'm not a member of any organized political party: I'm a Democrat!"[11]

The EU's structure is perhaps the best possible way to create a supranational democracy out of the great variety of democratic nations that have chosen to join. No nation will join the EU if it thinks it will be worse off for doing so, and since the core fear of any nation joining a supranational democracy is that it will be steamrollered by the other nations, a near-prerequisite for any supranational European democracy is unanimity rule. Without something close to a unanimity rule—at least for the big decisions—the EU would not exist. That means that pundit-driven proposals to shift the EU far closer to majority rule are fanciful—flights of pure theory as likely to work as a perpetual motion machine.

The Calculus of Unanimous Consent

Unanimity decision rules make governing difficult. It's a world where the squeakiest wheel gets the most grease and one hold-out can stop a good deal from happening. I know about this first-hand as a former staffer in the U.S. Senate, where much legislative activity happens by unanimous consent ("UC" in local parlance) and where even more *potential* legislation never gets introduced because everyone knows there's this one senator who doesn't like that one issue. The old tactic of filibustering a bill—talking without interruption to prevent a motion to bring the bill to the floor—is the most famous version of unanimity rule in the Senate. I strongly recommend James Stewart's performance in *Mr. Smith Goes to*

Washington, a black-and-white film from 1939, to give a sense of what that traditional form of unanimity rule looked like. But the real-world version of unanimity rule, in glorious Technicolor, isn't nearly as charming to watch.

The U.S. Senate isn't the only place with elements of unanimity rule. Poland's legislature in the 1600s and 1700s had it as well. Just by shouting the phrase *Nie pozwalam!* any legislator could stop any bill from becoming law. This is widely credited with exacerbating the political weakness of Poland. W. J. Wagner noted decades ago in the *Polish Review*, "Certainly, there was no other institution of old Poland which has been more sharply criticized in more recent times than this one."[12]

Some political thinkers, however, have had a soft spot for unanimity rule; even Wagner himself did. Unanimity is a way to guarantee that no government decision knowingly hurts any voter. If our primary concern in creating a government is to ensure that nobody is made worse off by a government decision—to ensure the decision is "Pareto efficient," as an economist would say—then one way to be sure nobody is hurt by a policy is to ask everybody if they agree to it. This was Swedish economist Knut Wicksell's thought, and he made just this point in his *Finanztheoretische Untersuchungen* (*Inquiries into Finance Theory*).[13] If government makes exploitation possible in principle, then let's get everyone's consent in practice to make sure that no one is being exploited.

My late colleague at George Mason University, the Nobel laureate James Buchanan, was the first person to translate a key portion of Wicksell's *Inquiries* into English. It appears that in reading it, he found much worth reflecting on and much worth arguing with. In an influential book that Buchanan coauthored with my late colleague Gordon Tullock, they argued that unanimous agreement had elements of a noble ideal because it really is important to reduce the probability that government action could make people worse off. But Buchanan and Tullock also emphasized that coming to agreement is just hard, even on the easiest of subjects.

An entire chapter of their famed *Calculus of Consent* is entitled "The Rule of Unanimity," and the ethics, merits, and downsides of unanimity rule are a recurring theme throughout their book.[14] They are clear that unanimity is a worthy ideal, one worth using as a starting point for serious political thinking, even if wise governments end up making decisions with less than the unanimous consent of the governed. The barrier to unanimity rule turns out to be the high cost of reaching agreement:

> The introduction of decision-making costs is required before any departure from the adherence to the unanimity rule can be rationally supported. . . . If costs of decision-making could be reduced to negligible proportions, the rational individual should always support the requirement of unanimous consent before political decisions are finally made.[15]

Buchanan and Tullock were particularly concerned that under majority rule, minorities would become victims, and that the majority might often vote to impose "external costs" (bad side effects) on the minority: "Moreover, [under majority rule,] so long as there exist minorities who disagree with the decisions reached, some external costs will be expected . . . only the unanimity rule will insure that all external effects will be eliminated."[16] Their particular example was the question of how to divide a nation's oil wealth. Under majority rule, it's easy to imagine 51% of the people agreeing that a particular 51% of the people should get 100% of the oil wealth. And certainly that example has mattered in real-world settings in resource-rich countries. But the metaphor is much broader, just as the parable of the Good Samaritan applies even thousands of miles away from the Levant.

Our modern expectation that group decisions—democratic decisions—are majoritarian by default is, according to Buchanan and Tullock, a mistake. Instead of starting with 50% + 1 and occasionally working up from there, they think we should start at 100% and, only with some reluctance, work *down* from there: "In political discussion . . . many scholars seem to have overlooked the central place that the unanimity rule must occupy in any normative theory of democratic government."[17]

The conclusion that Buchanan, Tullock, and Wicksell came to by reflecting on the human tendency to exploit other humans, the EU came to by necessity. If you want a nation to voluntarily join the EU, that nation probably needs to feel that it can reject any EU decision that would make it massively worse off. But regardless of how the EU came to the need for frequent unanimity rule, *unanimity rule is certainly democratic*. The question of whether unanimity rule is wise or efficient is quite distinct from this separate question of whether it's democratic. Thus, complaints about the EU's unanimity rule—and its more frequently used supermajority alternative, qualified majority rule—are complaints about the type of democracy you're living under. They're not complaints about whether you're living in a democracy or an oligarchy. Europeans might feel out of touch with the decisions of the EU Council, but when they do they're feeling out of touch with a democratic decision.

So how often should democracies choose unanimity rule? As Buchanan and Tullock emphasize in theory and as the history of Poland shows in practice, unanimity rule is costly and can lead to bad decisions. It's well understood within the EU that nations leaning toward a "no" vote are bought off with side payments—targeted farm subsidies, perhaps, or a shiny new EU office building to be built in a recalcitrant country. Such side payments are one practical method of "coming to unanimous agreement" that Buchanan and Tullock themselves discuss. If 90% of the people at the party want to order so-called pineapple pizza badly enough, and if the party can order only one kind of pizza, then even under unanimity rule, those 90% will probably be able to buy off the consent of the wise minority who are rightly skeptical of this pineapple-bread monstrosity. And if the 90% can't buy off the consent of the wise holdouts, that's a strong sign that the supermajority isn't all that excited about ordering their poor excuse for a pizza.

This line of reasoning—a version of the Nobel-winning Coase theorem—is officially an argument for how unanimity *can* work, but in practice it's an argument for just how hard it is to make unanimity work. Isn't buying off recalcitrant holdouts a poor use of time and money? And won't voters (or small European countries) have a strong incentive to play up their complaints—to exaggerate how much they dislike a piece of proposed legislation—just to extract the biggest side payment? Yes and yes. And the EU is a particularly strong example of the high cost of reaching unanimous consent. In a region with such high cultural diversity, with relatively religious countries in the East and relatively secular countries in the North and West, with nuclear families and strong individualism in the North and West and stronger, multi-generational family structures more common in the East and South, and economic differences everywhere, this is a formula for disagreement—both sincere disagreement and, well, let's call it "economically motivated disagreement."

Alas, the EU has the only kind of structure possible—one with strong elements of unanimity and supermajority rule—but that form of democracy will create inefficient haggling and too many fragile, unenforceable, largely ceremonial "agreements."

The Efficiency of Eurocracy Unleashed

The EU's democratic structures may have a tough time coming to agreement, but when they finally do agree on something and hand it off for enforcement, enforce the EU does.

The European Central Bank is an example. Economists weren't very supportive of the idea of creating the euro. If you'd held a vote in the 1990s among international monetary economists—experts on exchange rates, inflation, shared currencies, and the like—there's no doubt they'd have voted against creating a single currency shared among over a dozen European countries. There's a standard set of arguments for when a group of nations *should* share a single currency—a set of arguments made by Canadian Nobelist Robert Mundell—and the euro area didn't (and still doesn't) meet the requirements.[18] The big three:

1. When the region gets hit by economic shocks, they should mostly be common shocks, hitting all countries about equally, not

special regional shocks that just hit "the farming countries" rather than, say, "the factory countries." You can't cut interest rates solely for one region, just as you can't typically send chemotherapy to just a single cancerous organ—and since the direct effects go everywhere, the side effects also show up everywhere. Central banking is economic crop dusting. Careful targeting isn't its strong suit; it works best when different regions have a lot in common.

2. Workers and machines should be able to move across national borders, so if and when a bad regional shock hits one area, workers and (eventually) machines can move from the hard-hit nations to the economically stronger ones. Within the United States, for instance, people used to move across states a lot during recessions—one sign the country was a good place for a shared single currency.

3. There should be a system of transfer payments that can help areas hit by regional shocks. You can call the transfer payments "targeted tax credits" if that's your thing, or call them "relief payments" or "Social Security bonus payments," or whatever else you like. The transfer payments are another way to make up for the fact that a single area-wide central bank can't target its stimulus, so if a regional shock hits, it would be good to have some way to keep the hard-hit region spending, or at least keep it out of the path of deeply worsening poverty.

The eurozone obviously fails to meet all three criteria: it has local shocks, little mobility, and no eurozone-wide social safety net. You can see why economic experts were euroskeptics from the start—with the interesting exception of Robert Mundell himself, the economist who created this list in the first place. I'll set aside Mundell's support for the euro, his optimism, as a topic that deserves a book of its own. Instead, consider what *Vox*'s Matt Yglesias had to say about the euro back in 2015:

> If you try to understand the eurozone as an economic policy idea, you'll quickly start to see that it's a pretty stupid idea. . . . [However, the Eurozone is] primarily a political project, not an economic

one. And despite the considerable problems with European economies, it gives every indication of succeeding in its political goal of
pushing deeper and deeper integration of European countries.[19]

Given the central goal of deeper political and social integration,
EU member states came to an agreement on the form of commom
currency, the euro. In 1992, they signed the Maastricht Treaty,
which set the stage for later monetary union; and this treaty was
ratified by all the democratically elected governments of the EU.
Economists predicted it would be difficult—economically and, indi-
rectly, politically—to handle a shock that hit one region of Europe
harder than another. And, wow, did economists ever turn out to be
right about that.

The European debt crisis hit southern Europe harder than northern Europe, East harder than West, and the ECB was faced with
precisely the unappealing menu of options that the euroskeptics
from the 1990s predicted. The ECB's creative response was a form
of targeted stimulus in the form of buying up government bonds
of the weakest euro economies, bonds that prudent central banks
typically avoid purchasing. This had the effect of cutting interest
rates for just a subset of economically weaker countries, effectively
increasing the supply of loans to those countries, pushing down their
interest rates, and making it easier for people and businesses in those
countries to borrow money.

The ECB found a way to do something economists had known
was possible in principle but risky in practice: cut interest rates in just
one part of a shared currency area. The big risk of this policy isn't
rampant inflation because the ECB can always wage a typical battle
against inflation by raising interest rates across the eurozone for a
while. The big risk instead is that now the ECB has started engaging
in fiscal policy, buying up risky government bonds when it's always
possible that one of those countries could decide to default on some
or all of its debt, as the Greek government did in 2011. If the countries all make good on those bonds, the ECB isn't out any money,

but if they default, that means that back when the ECB bought those bonds, it was unknowingly giving those countries a gift.

That's the difference between a loan and a gift: a loan is a gift you eventually give back. And the only way to find out if you gave a loan or a gift is to wait and see if you get repaid. I hope it all works out just fine, and in any case, it reminds us that when the EU democracy handed an EU bureaucracy a tough, risky, unappealing task to perform, this bureaucracy did an amazingly good job of it.

The Eurocratic Efficiency of Frontex

By contrast, the European migration crisis that began in full force in 2015 offered a textbook example of the EU's democratic weaknesses. The diverse set of nations in the EU (predictably) couldn't come to any serious agreement on how to enforce border security or how to care for the hundreds of thousands of new migrants who had arrived on boats crossing the Mediterranean just that year. The 2015 arrivals were part of a larger European phenomenon: in total "about 2 million migrants . . . arrived in Europe by crossing the Mediterranean Sea" between 2009 and 2018, according to Pew Research.[20] Clearly the EU needed to come to some sort of agreement regarding how to take care of the needs of arriving migrants and what policies to enact about future border security.

How would the EU's democratic organs come to a decision on such important, controversial issues? When the Council voted on migration issues, the typical voting rule had long been unanimity rule, as you'd expect on such a sensitive topic. But on a central vote in 2015—a refugee resettlement plan designed to allocate 160,000 refugees across EU nations—the EU abandoned the unanimity norm on migration issues and instead passed the bill through a qualified majority vote on the Council. *Politico* noted at the time:

> The pressure to move on the refugee issue has been building throughout the past week, leading ministers to use the political "nuclear option" of qualified majority voting to adopt the relocation scheme. The voting mechanism is common for less-controversial

measures, but has never been used for something as sensitive and divisive as refugee relocation.[21]

The ostensible quotas that were the fruit of that nonunanimous decision have never been enforced. An article a year later, entitled "EU Buries Migration Dispute for Now," reported:

> "Very clearly, last year's package doesn't work," another diplomat said, adding . . . EU leaders had "a frank discussion" when 27 of them met in Bratislava in September. "Many member states had a strong position and agreed that it would be better to have more flexible solutions," the diplomat said.[22]

So even when the EU's quasi-senate attempts to use (qualified) majority rule on paper, they find that they have to live with the unanimity rule in practice.

However, on border control, an element of immigration policy where the democratic organs of the EU have greater agreement, the EU bureaucracy is again responsive and largely effective. Over the past few years, the EU has slowly and quietly built up an astonishingly robust border control agency, Frontex. Frontex was officially created in the fall of 2015, the time of the failed refugee resettlement "agreement." European leaders knew they had a problem with border control—the predecessor to Frontex had done little—and so they created an agency that within a year had genuine power to enforce migration rules. Frontex's official name is the European Border and Coast Guard Agency. And while as of this writing it doesn't have a single border guard or coast-patrolling ship to its name, and instead relies on cooperation with European governments, current plans call for a Frontex with 10,000 border guards in just a few years. This is an enormous policy change, driven by democratic political demands but formally recommended by the technocratic European Commission itself.[23]

The Eurocracy has given the EU's democratic leaders just what they've asked for. Frontex, backed by the EU's new democratic consensus on immigration restriction, has apparently been effective at dramatically reducing migrant arrivals with arrival rates that by early 2017 fell below 20%, and closer to 10%, of their 2015 peaks. Sea arrivals per month had been over 150,000 in late 2015 and fell to an average of around 15,000 per month in early 2017.[24] This outcome appears to be what European voters want, according to numerous polls in late 2015 and since. As voter demands became clearer and citizens grew more vocal about their preference for lower migration levels, politicians responded, and the EC bureaucracy met most of the demands of EU voters.

A crucial method that Frontex uses to reduce migration flows is to work with African governments to reduce northward migration from sub-Saharan Africa toward Europe. This policy is known as "border externalization," and it often amounts to outsourcing government border enforcement to other countries, often countries with worse records on human rights. In an impassioned 2018 opinion piece, researcher Mark Akkerman writes, "Starting in 1992, but at an accelerated rate since 2015, the EU has pressurised third countries, mainly in Africa, to act as its border security outposts. . . . EU relations with African countries have become obsessively focused on stopping migration towards Europe, regardless of its consequences for forcibly displaced persons."[25]

As with the ECB's response to the debt crisis, Frontex has responded aggressively—many critics would say too aggressively—to the demands of its democratic bosses. The question of proper border control policy is far beyond the scope of this chapter, but the question of whether the EU's bureaucracy accomplishes the tasks that democratic politicians have handed it is well within its scope. And there is little doubt on this matter: by real-world standards, the EU's bureaucracy responds to voters. The EU has problems of democratic governance, but the problem is mostly with the democracy, not the governance.

9 Singapore: Flourishing with 50% Less Democracy

IN 2004, Harvard economist Lant Pritchett and the World Bank's Michael Woolcock asked, "What is the best way to get to 'Denmark?'"[1] By "Denmark" they didn't mean the affluent northern European country with a population of about 6 million. They meant competent governance, a government that routinely succeeds at providing "key services such as clean water, education, sanitation, policing, safety/sanitary regulation, roads, and public health[, all] assured by effective, rules-based, meritocratic, and politically accountable public agencies."[2]

Pritchett and Woolcock's paper contained what became a catchphrase for a key goal of economic development: "Getting to Denmark." The authors emphasize that Denmark is just a metaphor, and they also hint that there's another nation that would make for a similarly good metaphor: "By 'Denmark' we . . . mean the common core of the structure of the workings of the public sector in countries usually called 'developed' (including new arrivals like Singapore)."[3]

Singapore, an island nation in Southeast Asia, has about the same population as Denmark, an income per person that is about 80% higher than Denmark's, and a life expectancy that's two and a half years longer than Denmark's. So by some metrics, Singapore is better off—a bigger success story than Denmark. But these two small nations started off in quite different places in 1960—with Singapore starting off much the poorer of the two. Since 1960, Denmark has grown about four times richer per person, but over the same period, Singapore has grown about twenty-three times richer per person. At least by the metrics of income, life expectancy, and growth, it's worthy to discuss how to get to Denmark, but it's wise to discuss how to get to Singapore.

The Singapore miracle is economically impressive, and therefore politically impressive. However, its political miracle wasn't built on democracy, at least not according to any standard definition. Singapore definitely has elections, and by all accounts, its secret ballot votes are counted fairly. The Systemic Peace team—the good people who create the Polity index—note in their report on Singapore's political system:

> Multiparty elections have been a defining feature of the Singapore state since 1959. Despite these elections, the People's Action Party (PAP) has established a hegemonic one-party system . . . [and] the government has . . . used the threat of libel suits and its influence over the courts and the media to limit any significant challenge to PAP political hegemony.[4]

In Singapore, when you say the wrong things about government leaders, they don't throw you in jail: instead, as a rule, they sue you, and they win. That's enough to keep most political opposition inside the bounds that the PAP is comfortable with. Other tools are used as well—recently, strict permit requirements for public gatherings have turned into restrictions on social media discussions of Singaporean politics—so libel suits aren't the only mechanism Singapore uses to control political competition. It's well worth remembering that governments have a range of tools, some more brutal than others, and Singapore has generally avoided the most brutal tools.

Facing no substantial political competition—the PAP currently holds 82 out of 101 seats in the nation's parliament—and with the government wielding a great deal of control over the media,

Singapore surely fails to meet Nobel laureate Amartya Sen's minimal requirements for a democracy. You'll recall that Sen defined the level of democracy required to avoid a famine: genuinely competitive parties and a free media. Singapore fails both tests. That means that Singapore doesn't have 10% less democracy when compared to the world's rich democracies; it's certainly less democratic than that. Two widely used indexes point toward a useful, if still subjective, estimate: the Polity index discussed in Chapter 1 and the *Economist* magazine's Democracy Index.

The Democracy Index gives Singapore a 6.4 out of 10.0. The *Economist* calls Singapore a "flawed democracy"—the same category it gives to the United States, though the U.S. scores higher, at 8.0. The *Economist*'s index measure, however, isn't just an index of whether a nation *is* a democracy; it's also a measure of how well the democracy is functioning. That means that it places quite a lot of weight on performance measures, and not strictly on whether elections are competitive and whether votes are fairly counted. For example, the United States is downgraded in part because of a low score "in the *functioning of government* category, as political polarisation has become more pronounced and public confidence in institutions has weakened."[5] By comparison, the median "full democracy" in their index has a score of approximately 9, and the lowest score is approximately 1. By the *Economist*'s measure, Singapore is about 35% less democratic than the world's rich democracies—but again, that measure includes the results of democracy, not just the procedures of it.

By contrast, the good people at the Systemic Peace project, discussed in Chapter 1, give Singapore a much lower score: a combined Polity score of just –2 on a +10 to –10 scale. There are plenty of countries at both ends of the Polity scale, so Singapore is truly 60% below the rich democracies on that scale. In averaging these two measures, let's put more weight on the more neutral Polity score, and let's call Singapore a case of 50% less democracy. That means that the Singapore model isn't one to fully emulate, at least not for today's rich democracies. The chance of a horrifying outcome, even if low to moderate—not famine as much as war or a demolition of civil liberties that could potentially lead to governments killing their own citizens—is too high to recommend the full Singapore model to the average rich democracy. Singapore has succeeded by most measures for over five decades, but just because it succeeded doesn't mean other countries can follow the same path and get the same results. Singapore has been lucky—and this isn't a book about luck.

But there's still much to learn from this exceptional nation-level case study. Let's spend a few minutes on this wondrous exception.

The Creator of Singapore

It's often said that there's more to Singapore's origin story than Lee Kuan Yew. He was Singapore's first prime minister, held the office from 1959 to 1990, and continued to retain substantial political influence until 2011. But even though he's not the whole story, let's focus on the late LKY (as he was universally known) all the same—in part because he's so quotable.

LKY knew that voter skills shaped government quality:

> In new countries, democracy has worked and produced results only when there is an honest and effective government, which means a people smart enough to elect such a government. Remember, elected governments are only as good as the people who choose them. [1988]⁶

He emphasized that elections are a means to the end of creating good governance, and good governance requires effective leaders; but democratic elections might not be the best way to find those leaders:

> The problem now is how to work the system of one man, one vote when we have to get quality leadership to the top. If we leave it to natural processes it will be a contest on television performances as in the West. And the best television performers and rally entertainers are not necessarily the best leaders who can deliver good government. [1996]⁷

And having started with such a poor nation—he entitled his memoirs *From Third World to First*—LKY never took a rich Singapore for granted:

> We cannot afford to forget that public order, personal security, economic and social progress and prosperity are not the natural order of things, that they depend on ceaseless effort and attention from honest and effective government that the people must elect. [2000][8]

The Semidemocracy of Singapore

William F. Case of the University of Nottingham used an apt term for Singapore back in 1996: he called it a *semidemocracy*. He notes that Singapore holds real elections, but the PAP ensures that its core constituency—the middle class, not the traditional affluent elites, not the poor—has the greatest voice in society: "Thus, in Singapore core elites keep their grip on state power by spreading limits on liberal participation evenly across classes, then holding regular elections. At the same time, they favor the middle class by opening some side channels [for dialogue with the government]."[9]

What are these side channels, these mechanisms to make sure that the middle classes feel that they're actually being listened to? Case describes them: "Numerous forums for dialogue including the Feedback Unit, created in 1985, the Government Parliamentary Committees, introduced in 1987, and the Institute of Policy Studies, formed in 1988, have grown up alongside new middle class constituencies and dissuaded them from seeking more autonomous modes of participation."[10]

It's PAP's political ground game, designed to make the middle classes feel that they're being heard. And indeed, it gives the PAP more information about what the middle classes actually want. It's not democracy—it's not listening carefully to everyone. Instead it's semidemocracy: listening carefully to PAP's core constituency, but holding honest elections so that everyone can let off some steam.

The Wisdom of Singapore

Traveling to a country for a few days is no way to learn what it's really like. That obvious caveat aside, I've been to Singapore twice—once as a tourist, once to give an academic talk—and both visits were fantastic. The Night Safari at the Singapore Zoo is not to be missed. The roar of a distant lion; wandering through an aviary and walking within inches of a large fruit bat hanging at shoulder height; wallabies wandering up in another aviary-style enclosure. And Kaya toast—toast spread with a sweet coconut-egg jam—is a breakfast delight worth a trip in itself. But those brief trips didn't show me the nature of the Singaporean miracle. I learned much more about the country by looking at statistics, comparing it to other countries, and reading histories of the nation. That's how I've learned that although Singapore has perhaps 50% less democracy than the world's richest democracies, it built its miracle by using some of the same channels we've discussed.

First, **Singapore has exceptionally smart citizens: it has among the very highest average test scores in the world. In practice, Singapore already has an element of epistocracy.**

A purely anecdotal illustration: my first day in Singapore, I grabbed the newspaper. It contained an interview with a top government official who was describing the expansion of Changi Airport, and in the interview, the official said the government was interested in how many positive externalities the airport created. Now, externality is a term that in my experience rarely comes up outside of economics classes—it's our word for "side effect," like how my home's market value would rise if my neighbors took care of their lawn and stopped playing loud music after 9:00 p.m.[11] But I just don't hear that word in common usage. For instance, I'd never dare to include it in a draft of a Senate speech or in an op-ed. But the Singaporean official used the term without explanation. My later experience confirmed the anecdote: politicians in Singapore routinely discuss policy at an extremely high intellectual level, even in the newspapers. That's a sign that Singapore might be more than a semidemocracy: it may be the world's first semiepistocracy.

Second, Singapore has an independent-enough judiciary to receive high ratings from both the World Justice Project and the World Bank's Rule of Law Index.

Indeed, in the World Bank index, Singapore was ranked eighth in the world in 2017, just two behind Denmark. According to the World Justice Project, Singapore was thirtieth in the world in 2019, the highest in Asia, while Denmark was first in the world. Either way, Singapore has a high-quality legal system by current global standards.

How about Singapore's monetary policy? Alas, it's not independent at all of the political system; the current head of the Singapore Monetary Authority is also the nation's deputy prime minister, the popular Tharman Shanmugaratnam. But given the semidemocracy of Singapore, the nation's central bank is surely insulated from the voice of the voters.

Third, Singaporean electoral terms are reasonably long—four to five years—but that's just the term length that's written down on paper.

As we've seen, LKY held power for decades, and the tradition of long service has continued among Singapore's political elite. These are men and women with long time horizons—a feature that's all too rare among leaders in democracies.

Fourth, there's no doubt that the PAP is a highly effective political machine.

Indeed, the middle-class listening committees of Singapore sound like a modern version of Plunkitt's glee club, a glue that sticks voters to the PAP machine. Singapore has embraced political realism.

By these measures, it looks like Singapore's low-democracy path was simultaneously a path to greater prosperity. I can't suggest that your nation take the path all the way to Singapore—rich democracies have too much to lose if things go wrong—but perhaps your nation should take a good long walk down that road.

CONCLUSION
Buying the Right Dose of Democracy

Alexander Hamilton believed in political *science*. In the ninth of the *Federalist Papers*, he wrote:

> The science of politics . . . like most other sciences, has received great improvement. The efficacy of various principles is now well understood, which were either not known at all, or imperfectly known to the ancients. The regular distribution of power into distinct departments . . . [compare to Chapter 3 of this book]. The institution of courts composed of judges holding their offices during good behaviour [compare to Chapter 4—and the long terms of Chapter 2]. The representation of the people in the legislature, by deputies of their own election [perhaps compare Chapter 2; this is no celebration of direct democracy]. These are either wholly new discoveries, or have made their principal progress towards perfection in modern times. They are means, and powerful means, by which the excellencies of republican government [i.e., representative democracy] may be retained, and its imperfections lessened or avoided. [punctuation added.]

You'll also recall from Chapter 6 that Alexander Hamilton, first U.S. treasury secretary, also believed that government bondholders are "generally speaking, enlightened men." So Chapters 3, 4, and 6 of this book, and perhaps even Chapter 2, are Hamiltonian in spirit. Hamilton was no defender of 100% pure democracy. In his own way, different from my own, he was looking for the top of the democracy Laffer curve to balance the benefits of citizen influence against the benefits of keeping power from the people, keeping institutions independent of the immediate demands of voters.

Like Hamilton, I'm a believer in the science of politics. Political science exists whenever and wherever people who think about political issues pay close attention to the marriage of theory and data. For the previous nine chapters, I've attempted to create that marriage, to test ideas old and new about how to reform governance in today's rich democracies. In Hamilton's day, those who studied the science of politics had to test their ideas by reviewing case studies—a few anecdotal examples of nations that tried monarchy or independent judges or some other reform. Anecdotes ruled the world of political debate.

Since World War II, the rise of dozens of affluent democracies around the world, along with the rise of widespread data collection by governments, think tanks, businesses, and universities, makes it possible to test claims about government reform more thoroughly than ever before. We can say more about what makes for good governance than Hamilton ever could. Perhaps that's because our theories are better than those available to him—in particular I'm glad to celebrate the value of game theory, a great creation of twentieth-century social science—but mostly it's because we have more data.

What theories do the data support? And what reform proposals might flow from these results?

• Longer terms make for at least slightly braver, more technocratically oriented, less populist politicians. Based on this finding, I suggest that countries with two- or three-year legislative terms should consider at least four-year terms.

• Less democratic central banks are close to a free lunch—lower inflation, fewer banking crises. The rich nations have largely embraced independent central banks, but as Chapter 3 noted, just because the bank is independent on paper doesn't mean it's independent in practice. Top elected officials need to support central bank independence during good times and bad or else independence can become de jure but not de facto. The battle for independence is never fully won.

• Judges and regulatory agencies are likely to get better results when kept a little further from voters—and a less democratic, more oligarchical judiciary is particularly valuable. The downside risks to such reforms are low and the benefits high.

• Giving a little more weight to more informed groups of voters, especially in the upper house of a national legislature, might be just the epistocratic nudge that representative democracy needs.

More speculatively, though with speculation driven by social science theory and useful analogies, we might further conclude:

• Government bondholders are one group that cares a lot about your nation's long-run profitability. It may be time to treat them more like government shareholders—voting rights and all. They're already tacitly influencing your government's policies, so it may be time to bring them explicitly into the halls of power. They probably have some good ideas.

• With the rise of high-hostility, polarizing social media, the voice of the citizen is a lot noisier than before. It may be wise to let party insiders have a bit more influence over party politics, as Jonathan Rauch of Brookings rightly suggests.

• Most speculative of all, somewhat more frequent, lower-stakes elections could reduce the influence of the media-outrage-of-the-month on government policy—electing half of a nation's parliament every three years rather than the entire parliament every six, for instance. Here, the U.S. Senate has the right idea, with a third of the members running every two years. Stability in the councils of power is wise when the electorate is, well, less than wise.

Would a government that embraced many of these reforms still be "democracies"? I'm not one for worrying about definitions and precise jargon, but since this particular word has meant so much to so many, let's take a moment to weigh the many meanings of *democracy* over the centuries and compare it to other prominent alternative forms of government. That should help us understand whether the governments we have and whether the governments we want are 100% democratic.

Like James Madison, his *Federalist Papers* coauthor, Hamilton knew that in his age, the word *democracy* had a negative ring to it. Both he and Madison used the word *republic* to refer to what we now call representative democracy—elected officials who to some degree represent the will of the voters. And Madison and Hamilton were clear about the difference between a democracy and a republic. They typically saved the word democracy to refer to what Madison in *Federalist No. 10* called "a pure democracy, by which I mean, a society consisting of a small number of citizens, who assemble and administer the government in person." In the same essay, Madison, like Hamilton, uses *republic* to mean what we routinely call "representative democracy": "A republic, by which I mean a government in which the scheme of representation takes place, opens a different prospect, and promises the cure for which we are seeking. Let us examine the points in which it varies from pure democracy."

Hamilton and Madison emphasized throughout the *Federalist Papers* that the U.S. Constitution, then awaiting ratification by the thirteen states, was no plan for "pure democracy." Instead, the Constitution was a plan for something else: a government with some elements of oligarchy—especially in the Senate, whose members were selected by state legislatures, not by voters—and with some elements of monarchy—particularly with a powerful president chosen by an electoral college, a college originally somewhat like the college of cardinals who in Rome come together to select the elective monarch known as the pope. And the mixed monarchical-oligarchical element of the judiciary—with appointments for life "during good behaviour"—while not emphasized in the past has become more obvious in the subsequent centuries.

One hundred percent pure democracy was never on the menu of the moderns. The word *democracy* reminded Enlightenment-era thinkers on both sides of the Atlantic of ancient Athens in particular, a city with many extremely intelligent people, great wealth, and a large overseas empire that nevertheless both lost the Peloponnesian War to nearly totalitarian Sparta and also voted to kill the great philosopher Socrates. If Athens is your best case for democracy, many enlightened thinkers concluded, maybe democracy is overrated. And once the French Revolution, Reign of Terror and all, became the next famed example of something ostensibly approaching pure democracy, the price of shares in pure democracy tanked, and have yet to recover.

Democracy Plus Oligarchy: A Time-Honored Recipe for Better Government

Other political thinkers across the centuries had already concluded that the best form of government was surely not pure democracy but something that combined elements of democracy, aristocracy (rule by the best, the most virtuous, not just the richest), and perhaps monarchy. Aristotle, Polybius, and Machiavelli, in the fourth century BCE, second century BCE, and fifteenth century CE, respectively, all came by different paths to much the same conclusion. At the same time, each writer emphasized that each of these three forms of government had an evil version—a Mr. Hyde to the Dr. Jekyll—which could erupt unpredictably. Democracy could become mob rule, aristocracy (rule by the best) could become oligarchy (rule by a few for the benefit of that few), and monarchy (largely benevolent rule focused on the long run) could become tyranny (Saddam Hussein).

One of the many strengths of premodern political thought is that its finest exemplars rarely assume the can opener of competent government. They begin with the opposite assumption: that people and governments are flawed and proceed from there. There's no great villain who must be defeated once and for all in the third act; there's no final boss battle after which a golden age of governance will arise. It's all just muddling through, an ongoing struggle against the forces of institutional decay.

Aristotle, a student of Plato who in turn was a student of the ill-fated Socrates, emphasized that some sort of balance was likely to lead to better government:

> If I was right when I said in the [Nicomachean] *Ethics* that . . . goodness consists in a mean, it follows that the best way of life is a mean, a mean which can be attained by everyone. These same criteria must be used to judge the excellence or otherwise of a constitution, which is, so to speak, the life of a state . . . Every state has three parts: the very rich, the very poor, and the middle class.[1]

Aristotle spends some time elaborating on the merits of the middle class—the "mean" or average class. He says they tend to listen to reason (compare Chapter 5), they are enough like each other that friendliness and social equality are more likely to arise, and compared to the poor and rich, respectively, they're more likely to pay taxes and less likely to covet government power. Aristotle concludes, "Therefore, of course, a state which rests upon the middle class is the best constituted in respect of those elements which, in our opinion, constitute a state. . . . All this goes to show that the best political society is one where power lies with the middle class."[2]

But not every state can hand power solely to the middle class. In Aristotle's day, that was partly because many states didn't have a big enough middle class, and in our modern age, it's partly because of the cultural norm of near-universal suffrage in democracies. When inequality is extreme, Aristotle sees little hope: "In those democracies which have no middle class and the poor far outnumber the rich, trouble ensues and the state soon goes to pieces."[3]

So having a lot of fairly affluent, reasonable citizens is a good way to go. However, if the poor (whom today we might call "working class") or the rich are more powerful, what's a good alternative, maybe the best alternative? Again, a form of balance, but a different balance, one that Aristotle calls *polity*: "Polity may be described generally as a fusion of oligarchy and democracy; but the term is most often used of those constitutions which incline toward democracy."[4]

What counted as oligarchy in Aristotle's day? He offers this example, one that many people today, including me, would consider extremely democratic: "The appointment of magistrates . . . by the process of election . . . is looked upon as oligarchical."[5] In Aristotle's day, people took democracy—direct participation of citizens—quite literally.

Let's run with the concept of polity. How will we know if it's working fairly well? Aristotle, who frequently dissects definitions to the granular level, upends our expectations in this case. He says we'll know the polity is working well when we can't precisely define it: "One criterion of a satisfactory blend of oligarchy with democracy is the possibility of describing a single constitution both (1) as a democracy and (2) as an oligarchy."[6]

So a satisfactory polity sounds a lot like a modern "democracy": the masses are involved, and yet it's obvious that insiders have a lot of influence as well. And it appears that to Aristotle, that's a good thing: the oligarchs and the masses balance each other, simulating the benefits of a dominant middle class. The combination of mass involvement in political questions with additional, crucial roles for your nation's elite; that's what Aristotle called *polity* and what we— you and me together—can quite gladly call *democracy*. Modest shifts in the balance, 10% one way or another, won't change that.

Diversifying the Constitutional Portfolio

Polybius, a Greek historian who studied the history of the Roman republic amid its golden age, is famed for emphasizing that a mixed form of government is best, though his recipe is different from Aristotle's. Polybius notes that "most of those who profess to give us authoritative instruction on this subject [the best form of government] distinguish three kinds of constitutions, which they designate kingship, aristocracy, democracy."[7]

But Polybius held a low opinion of "most of those" ancient experts—who, he says, insisted on choosing just one of the three options. In that respect, Polybius has a lot in common with Wallace Shawn's Vizzini, the arrogant, incompetent kidnapper in *The Princess Bride*: "Have you ever heard of Plato, Aristotle, Socrates? . . . Morons!"

Polybius explains where he thinks his predecessors went wrong: "For it is plain that we must regard as the best constitution that which partakes of all these three elements."[8] He then goes on to provide evidence for his argument by offering historical anecdotes. While Polybius's mind was in the right place, he lacked the evidence and the empirical methods to test his case carefully.

And so too with Machiavelli. In his *Discourses*, longer and more democracy-focused than his more famous *The Prince*, Machiavelli largely takes the Polybius position, and like Polybius he uses historical anecdotes as his key evidence. After mentioning the noble big three—democracy, aristocracy, and monarchy—and their evil twins—anarchy, oligarchy, and tyranny—Machiavelli says, "Let me say, therefore, that all the forms of government listed are defective: the three good ones because of the brevity of their lives, and the three bad ones because of their inherent harmfulness."[9]

So government-by-casserole (throwing a little of everything into the mix) turns out to be the solution: "Thus, those who were prudent in establishing laws recognized this fact and, avoiding each of these forms in themselves, chose one that combined them all, judging such a government to be steadier and more stable, for when there is in the same city-state a principality, an aristocracy, and a democracy, one form keeps watch over the other."[10]

Note that Machiavelli emphasizes a checks-and-balances story: keeping watch over each other and celebrating political rivalry as a path to government oversight. In the previous nine chapters, I've emphasized paths that were different from Machiavelli's, but he and

I have come to similar conclusions: pure democracy is not an ideal to strive for; it's a mistake to be avoided. And unlike Machiavelli's theory of how to reform government, mine doesn't rely on ancient anecdotes of doubtful accuracy.

Testing Robert Dahl

Within traditional political science, Yale's Robert Dahl was surely the greatest theorist of democracy of the late twentieth century. I particularly loved his short book *Who Governs?*[11] It offers a nearly anthropological overview of how local government really worked in New Haven, Connecticut, Yale's hometown. Dahl wrote many thoughtful books about democracy, but it's safe to say that *On Democracy*[12] was his mature reflection on the merits of representative democracy, which he often preferred to call *polyarchy*. In his fifth chapter, he frames his case for democracy, breaking it down into ten elements. I'll reorganize them here.

This one he's right about: *Avoiding tyranny.*

One indicator of tyrannical rule is when the government murders those it governs. As we saw in Chapter 1, democracies, as measured by conventional political rights indexes, rarely kill their own citizens. But recall that a nation only has to be in the top 25% of a democratic rights index to have a nearly perfect record of not killing its own citizens. On this issue at least, a modest dose of democracy appears to go a long way. And even though we can't be sure that this correlation is caused by greater democracy itself, given the stakes, this is a reasonable time for Dumbo to hold onto that feather. The next questions become: What is the right dose of democracy? And how much does a high dose cost?

Dahl next turns to a more ambiguous benefit of democracy: *Political equality.*

He wrestles for quite some time with the question of whether it's a net benefit at all since he is well aware that in the real world, people aren't equally capable of adding value to the political discourse. With the widening debate in favor of epistocracy in recent years, it's safe to say that the case for exact, universal political equality at the ballot box is weaker than it was when Dahl wrote his books—and that's just as it should be.

The next category of alleged benefits of "democracy" relies heavily on an oligarchical, nearly monarchical judiciary:

General freedom

Protecting essential personal interests

Self-determination

Moral autonomy

Essential rights

When it comes to personal freedoms, civil rights, and self-determination, it's the judges whom we trust the most in modern democracies, not the voting citizens, not the legislatures. An appeal to human rights is likely to be an appeal for less democracy, not more.

And in the last three categories, it's hard to tell whether democracy is driving the outcomes at all:

Human development

Peace seeking

Prosperity

As we saw in Chapter 1, there's no consensus at all on whether mass voter involvement makes nations richer and more peaceful, whether the causation is partly reversed—perhaps democracy is a luxury good often purchased by wealthy nations—or whether some third force—let's call it the force of liberalism—helps create both the conditions leading to peace and conditions that lead to prosperity.

Dahl was a genuinely wise scholar, and I recommend his armchair reflections on the value of democracy. I've learned an enormous amount from him. But once we take Dahl's reflections to the data, the case for maximal democracy weakens—and slightly less democracy looks affordable, even appealing.

The Liberalism-Democracy Trade-Off

Liberalism in the European sense—equal personal, social, and religious rights for citizens; a strong presumption of personal freedom; a high degree of economic freedom; and very likely a robust social safety net—is no friend of pure democracy. Voters are impetuous, shortsighted, frequently fail to see the invisible hand, and are typically supportive of the social status quo. And while pure democracy isn't a live option today, representative democracy is. But as we've seen, representative democracy isn't the best option for the judiciary: elected judges are less effective than appointed judges. And since the judiciary is the best guarantor of many of the liberties that make up liberalism, pro-democratic reforms that strengthen the link between judges and citizens are likely to weaken liberalism.

So if a modern, relatively prosperous nation wants a greater degree of liberalism, it probably wants at least a little less democracy. Impure democracy should always be the starting point for debate, and from there the wise will debate which level of impurity is best. Should France become 8% more impure? Should Japan become 12% more impure? The precise answer matters less than the general direction of reform, since the science of politics is like the science of optimal medicine dosage: approximation, not exactitude. Wise political reformers will follow the advice of philosopher Carveth Read: "It is better to be vaguely right than exactly wrong."[13]

Most prominent political thinkers either take the unalloyed merits of democracy for granted or call whatever institutional reforms they prefer "true democracy." When most thinkers are making those sorts of mistakes, the contrarian approach of just being vaguely right about democracy—by never assuming that "Democracy = The Good," and by combining good theory and modern empirical methods—will be one giant leap for good institutional reform.

Buying the Right Dose of Democracy

I encourage you to support a level of democracy consistent with your personal morality. If your personal morality dictates universal suffrage, mandatory voting, three-year terms for legislators, and smartphone plebiscites for changes in the rate of income tax, then that's the level of democracy you should support. Perhaps the best option is to just stick with the moral views you currently have and then consider the range of reform options permitted by your personal morality—reforms that might include:

- Requiring college degrees to vote in elections—but only to the upper house of parliament
- Eliminating elected judges—and elected treasurers
- Six-year terms for the nation's president

The next step: Taking your morality as given, start weighing the benefits and costs of different reform options.

Of course, there's another path, the reverse path:

First, consider the costs and benefits of the many democracy-reducing reforms I've suggested throughout this book. Then use those reforms as a springboard to think of more possible reforms of your own.

Second, after you've considered the merits and weaknesses of slightly less democracy, take some time to reflect on how much your personal morality will cost you. Find out which promising reforms would run afoul of your current moral worldview.

With some confidence, I can assure you that the benefits of 10% less democracy will be large—large enough that you just might be tempted to switch to a more flexible, more affordable morality.

Acknowledgments

I owe an enormous debt to my colleagues in George Mason University's economics department. They began shaping my intellectual world long before I came to Mason. I devoured Walter Williams's newspaper columns as a teenager; read James Buchanan, Richard Wagner, and Gordon Tullock's books as a graduate student; and began reading Tyler Cowen and Alex Tabarrok's influential blog *Marginal Revolution* during in its early weeks.

The first post at Marginal Revolution was by Tabarrok, posted in August 2003, and it was entitled "The Lunar Men." It described a number of great minds of Enlightenment England, including "Erasmus Darwin, Matthew Boulton, James Watt, Josiah Wedgwood," and others, who "met regularly under the light of the full moon to talk science." At GMU we meet for lunch or drop by each other's offices rather than meet under the moon, but it's no exaggeration to say that the level of scientific discussion in GMU's economics department rivals that of those long-ago sublunar meetings. My colleagues have improved my mind over twelve years at GMU, and for that I will always owe them my gratitude.

I first had the opportunity to lecture on the topic of 10% less democracy at the university's economics undergraduate club, the Economics Society, in 2015. I'm exceptionally grateful for the invitation:

that lecture taught me that our culture's nearly data-free obsession with ever greater democracy was a barrier to understanding good government. I also thank Southern Methodist University's O'Neil Center for Global Markets and Freedom for inviting me to speak on the ideas surrounding this book, as well as GMU's Center for Study of Public Choice and Dan Klein's Invisible Hand Seminar for offering me the opportunity to lecture on an early draft of the book. I particularly thank the Center for Study of Public Choice for financially supporting my work on this book.

I'm also grateful to John Nye, Mark Koyama, Cesar Martinelli, Arnold King, Dan Klein, Noel Johnson, Tim Kane, Daniel Klein, Jon Jorgensen, and Amy Cody for their insightful discussions and intellectual inspiration. Robin Hanson deserves particular thanks for suggestions about the chapter on the European Union, Tim Groseclose for his comments about real-world legislatures, and Tabarrok for suggestions regarding the epistocracy and independent agency chapters. I would like to thank my GMU colleague Jane Perry for her editing suggestions. I owe my friends Matt DeVries, Tanya DeCell, and Karen Johnson many thanks for thoughtful comments regarding early drafts. All remaining errors are, of course, those of Matt DeVries, my lifelong friend and muse.

My first editor at Stanford University Press, Margo Beth Fleming, taught me how to write a book, and I continue to learn from her. Steve Catalano, my editor who has faithfully guided 10% Less Democracy to completion, has been inordinately supportive and helpful. Sunna Juhn, Anne Fuzellier, and my exceptional copyeditor, Bev Miller, have made the final stages of editing and revision effortless, and for that I'm grateful. Two anonymous reviewers offered extremely insightful advice and valuable critiques.

I have written this book in the hope that my nieces and nephews—Sienna, Coco, Ethan, and Mac—will all be able to live under better, wiser, more foresighted governments: my love to you all.

Notes

Introduction

1. Natalie Schulhof, "'Less Democracy, Better Government,' Says Mason Professor," *Fourth Estate*, March 3, 2015, http://gmufourthestate.com/2015/03/03/less-democracy-better-government-says-mason-professor.

2. Ben Norton, "Koch-Funded Economist Wants 'Less Democracy,'" Counterpunch.org, March 27, 2015, https://www.counterpunch.org/2015/03/27/koch-funded-economist-wants-less-democracy/.

3. You might think that I'm saying good things about the senator because I want to keep the door open to some future position on the Hill; maybe everyone says nice things about their old Senate bosses. Cynicism is always appropriate in politics, but here are two reasons to believe me:

  1. In my experience, Hill staffers are pretty willing to talk about what their bosses are like. There's a kind of pride in having a stiff or arrogant or even mean senator telling you what to do all day long.

  2. Senator Hatch retired in 2019 after forty years in the Senate; he was then president pro tempore, the most senior member of the majority party, when he retired. And once a senator is gone, the value of any political connections you have with that particular senator diminishes quickly. A 2012 study published in a leading economics journal reported the authors' key finding: "lobbyists connected to US senators suffer an average 24 percent drop in generated revenue when their previous employer leaves the Senate." Jordi Blanes i Vidal, Mirko Draca, and Christian Fons-Rosen,

"Revolving Door Lobbyists," *American Economic Review* 102, no. 7 (2012): 3731–3748. So an evidence-based cynic will realize I have a much weaker financial incentive to say nice things about my old boss than I did last year. That raises the probability that I'm actually telling the truth.

Chapter 1

1. Amartya K. Sen, *Development as Freedom* (New York: Oxford University Press, 2001), 16.

2. William Easterly, Roberta Gatti, and Sergio Kurlat, "Development, Democracy, and Mass Killings," *Journal of Economic Growth* 11, no. 2 (2006): 137.

3. Seymour Martin Lipset, "Some Social Requisites of Democracy: Economic Development and Political Legitimacy," *American Political Science Review* 53 (1) (1959): 69–105.

4. John Gerring, Philip Bond, William T. Barndt, and Carola Moreno, "Democracy and Economic Growth: A Historical Perspective," *World Politics* 57, no. 3 (2005): 323. The fixed-effects regressions they discuss offer "before-and-after" evidence on democracy and growth.

5. Gerring et al., "Democracy and Economic Growth," 323–324.

6. Daron Acemoglu, Suresh Naidu, Pascual Restrepo, and James A. Robinson, "Democracy Does Cause Growth," *Journal of Political Economy* 127, no. 1 (2019): 47–100.

7. Robert A. Dahl, *On Democracy* (New Haven: Yale University Press, 1998), 38.

8. Mark S. Bell and Kai Quek, "Authoritarian Public Opinion and the Democratic Peace," *International Organization* 72, no. 1 (2018): 227.

9. Albert O. Hirschman, *The Passions and the Interests: Political Arguments for Capitalism Before Its Triumph* (Princeton: Princeton University Press, 1977), 14.

10. John R. Oneal and Bruce Russett, "Assessing the Liberal Peace with Alternative Specifications: Trade Still Reduces Conflict," *Journal of Peace Research* 36, no. 4 (1999): 423.

11. Håvard Hegre, "Democracy and Armed Conflict," *Journal of Peace Research* 51, no. 2 (2014): 159.

12. Håvard Hegre, Michael Bernhard, and Jan Teorell, "Reassessing

the Democratic Peace: A Novel Test Based on the Varieties of Democracy Data," working paper (2018), 1.

13.   Monty G. Marshall and Ted Robert Gurr, *Polity IV Project: Political Regime Characteristics and Transitions, 1800–2016. Dataset Users' Manual* (Vienna, VA: Center for Systemic Peace, 2017), 14.

14.   Marshall and Gurr, *Polity IV Project*, 15.

15.   Lee Hsiang Liow, Mikael Fortelius, Ella Bingham, Kari Lintulaakso, Heikki Mannila, Larry Flynn, and Nils Chr. Stenseth, "Higher Origination and Extinction Rates in Larger Mammals," *Proceedings of the National Academy of Sciences* 105, no. 16 (2008): 6097–6102.

16.   Jewel Stolarchuk, "'Buffet-Syndrome' Explanation Is 'Completely at Odds with Reality': SDP Chairman," *Independent* (Singapore), March 15, 2018, http://theindependent.sg/buffet-syndrome-explanation -is-completely-at-odds-with-reality-sdp-chairman/.

17.   Robert J. Barro, "Democracy and Growth," *Journal of Economic Growth* 1, no. 1 (1996): 14.

18.   The –1.6% result comes from Barro's dummy variable estimates— of low, medium, and high levels of democracy. Interpreting his quadratic democracy estimates, the move from a 0.5 democracy score on a 0–1 scale to a 1.0 democracy scores yields a –1.3% predicted effect on annual growth in income per person.

19.   Rafael Di Tella, Robert J. MacCulloch, and Andrew Oswald, "Preferences over Inflation and Unemployment: Evidence from Surveys of Happiness," *American Economic Review* 91, no. 1 (2001): 340.

20.   Gregory N. Mankiw, *Principles of Macroeconomics*, 8th ed. (Boston: Cengage, 2018).

21.   Robert J. Barro, "Inflation and Economic Growth," *Annals of Economics and Finance* 14, no. 1 (2013): 121–144.

22.   William Easterly, "National Policies and Economic Growth: A Reappraisal," in *Handbook of Economic Growth*, edited by Philippe Aghion and Steven Durlauf, vol. 1, pp. 1015–1059. New York: Elsevier, 2005.

23.   Benjamin F. Jones and Benjamin A. Olken, "Do Leaders Matter? National Leadership and Growth Since World War II," *Quarterly Journal of Economics* 120, no. 3 (2005): 835–864.

Chapter 2

1. David R. Mayhew, *Congress: The Electoral Connection* (New Haven: Yale University Press, 1974).

2. Frédéric Bastiat, "What Is Seen and What Is Not Seen," *Ideas on Liberty* 51 (2001): 12.

3. Kenneth A. Shepsle, Robert P. Van Houweling, Samuel J. Abrams, and Peter C. Hanson, "The Senate Electoral Cycle and Bicameral Appropriations Politics," *American Journal of Political Science* 53, no. 2 (2009): 343–359.

4. Ray C. Fair, "Presidential and Congressional Vote?Share Equations," *American Journal of Political Science* 53, no. 1 (2009): 59.

5. Fair reports that the t-statistics, a measure of the accuracy of a predicted forecasting relationship, is larger for election year economic growth than for the boom quarters.

6. "Trade Within Europe," IGM Forum, December 7, 2016.

7. "China-Europe Trade," IGM Forum, April 12, 2018.

8. Matthew F. Daley, Nicole Liddon, Lori A. Crane, Brenda L. Beaty, Jennifer Barrow, Christine Babbel, Lauri E. Markowitz et al., "A National Survey of Pediatrician Knowledge and Attitudes Regarding Human Papillomavirus Vaccination," *Pediatrics* 118, no. 6 (2006): 2280–2289, and Matthew F. Daley, Lori A. Crane, Lauri E. Markowitz, Sandra R. Black, Brenda L. Beaty, Jennifer Barrow, Christine Babbel et al., "Human Papillomavirus Vaccination Practices: A Survey of US Physicians 18 Months After Licensure," *Pediatrics* 126, no. 3 (2010): 425–433.

9. Paola Conconi, Giovanni Facchini, and Maurizio Zanardi, "Policymakers' Horizon and Trade Reforms: The Protectionist Effect of Elections," *Journal of International Economics* 94, no. 1 (2014): n. 3.

10. Conconi, Facchini, and Zanardi, "Policymakers' Horizon and Trade Reforms," 111.

11. Paola Conconi, David R. DeRemer, Georg Kirchsteiger, Lorenzo Trimarchi, and Maurizio Zanardi, "Suspiciously Timed Trade Disputes," *Journal of International Economics* 105 (2017): 57.

12. From two independent sources, I've heard a related story about a U.S. president's policy choice during a preelection trade dispute. The president in question chose to impose tariffs to help out a troubled industry just before an election, and both stories turn on how this president quite bluntly explained the cruel trade-off between good politics and

good economics to two different very good economists. The consilience in the tales, reported to quite different audiences years apart, I take as a sign that many leading politicians get the cruel trade-off between getting reelected and doing a good job of running a government.

13.   Stephanie J. Rickard and Teri L. Caraway, "International Negotiations in the Shadow of National Elections," *International Organization* 68, no. 3 (2014): 701–720.

14.   "France's Labor Market," IGM Forum, May 17, 2017.

15.   Responses in the IGM survey don't add up to 100% because "Did not answer" is also an option.

16.   Rickard and Caraway, "International Organizations," 710.

17.   Jeffry Frieden, Piero Ghezzi, and Ernesto Stein, "Politics and Exchange Rates: A Cross-Country Approach to Latin America," in *The Currency Game: Exchange Rate Politics in Latin America*, ed. Jeffry Frieden and Ernesto Stein (Baltimore, MD: Johns Hopkins University Press, 2009), 59.

18.   Mareike Kleine and Clement Minaudier, "Negotiating Under Political Uncertainty: National Elections and the Dynamics of International Co-Operation," *British Journal of Political Science* 49, no. 1 (2019): 315–337.

19.   Eduardo Alemán and Ernesto Calvo, "Analyzing Legislative Success in Latin America: The Case of Democratic Argentina," in *The Study of New Democracies in Latin America*, ed. Guillermo O'Donnell, Joseph Tulchin and Augusto Varas. with Adam Stubits (Washington, DC: Woodrow Wilson International Center for Scholars, 2008).

20.   Frank R. Baumgartner, Sylvain Brouard, Emiliano Grossman, Sebastien G. Lazardeux, and Jonathan Moody, "Divided Government, Legislative Productivity, and Policy Change in the USA and France," *Governance* 27, no. 3 (2014): 423–447.

21.   Kleine and Minaudier, "Negotiating Under Political Uncertainty," 2.

22.   Ernesto Dal Bó and Martín A. Rossi, "Term Length and the Effort of Politicians," *Review of Economic Studies* 78, no. 4 (2011): 1237–1263.

23.   Dal Bó and Rossi, "Term Length," 1238.

24.   Dal Bó and Rossi, "Term Length," 1237.

25.   Dal Bó and Rossi, "Term Length," 1239.

26. Rocio Titiunik, "Drawing Your Senator from a Jar: Term Length and Legislative Behavior," *Political Science Research and Methods* 4, no. 2 (2016): 293.

27. Robert Dahl, *On Democracy* (New Haven: Yale University Press, 1998)

Chapter 3

1. Alberto Alesina and Lawrence H. Summers, "Central Bank Independence and Macroeconomic Performance: Some Comparative Evidence," *Journal of Money, Credit and Banking* 25, no. 2 (1993): 151–162.

2. James Tobin, "On Improving the Economic Status of the Negro," in *The Negro American*, ed. Talcott Parsons and Kenneth Bancroft Clark (Boston: Houghton Mifflin, 1966), 457–458. See also Paul A. Samuelson and Robert M. Solow, "Analytical Aspects of Anti-Inflation Policy," *American Economic Review Papers and Proceedings* 50, no. 2 (1960): 177–194.

3. Alesina and Summers, "Central Bank Independence," 153.

4. Alesina and Summers, "Central Bank Independence," 153.

5. Alberto Posso and George B. Tawadros, "Does Greater Central Bank Independence Really Lead to Lower Inflation? Evidence from Panel Data," *Economic Modelling* 33 (2013): 244–247.

6. Alex Cukierman, *Central Bank Strategy, Credibility, and Independence: Theory and Evidence* (Cambridge, MA: MIT Press, 1992). Also see Vittorio Grilli, Donato Masciandaro, and Guido Tabellini, "Political and Monetary Institutions and Public Financial Policies in the Industrial Countries," *Economic Policy* 6, no. 13 (1991): 341–392.

7. Alesina and Summers, "Central Bank Independence," 159.

8. Alesina and Summers, "Central Bank Independence," 159.

9. Alex Cukierman, "Central Bank Independence and Policy Results: Theory and Evidence," lecture prepared for the Bank of Mexico international conference, "Stability and Economic Growth: The Role of the Central Bank," Mexico City, 2005.

10. Kenneth Rogoff, " The Optimal Degree of Commitment to an Intermediate Monetary Target," *Quarterly Journal of Economics* 100, no. 4 (1985): 1169–1189.

11. Finn E. Kydland and Edward C. Prescott, "Time to Build and Aggregate Fluctuations," *Econometrica* (1982): 1345–1370. Also see

John B. Long Jr. and Charles I. Plosser, "Real Business Cycles," *Journal of Political Economy* 91, no. 1 (1983): 39–69.

12.   Orson Scott Card, *Ender's Game* (New York: Tor Books, 1985).

13.   Jeroen Klomp and Jakob De Haan, "Central Bank Independence and Financial Instability," *Journal of Financial Stability* 5, no. 4 (2009): 321–338.

14.   Alberto Alesina and Andrea Stella, "The Politics of Monetary Policy," in *Handbook of Monetary Economics*, vol. 3, ed. Benjamin Friedman and Michael Woodford (Amsterdam: North-Holland, 2010), 1001–1054.

15.   Alan S. Blinder, *Central Banking in Theory and Practice* (Cambridge, MA: MIT Press, 1999), 56.

16.   Blinder, *Central Banking*, 55.

17.   Blinder, *Central Banking*, 56.

18.   James Duesenberry, "Comment on `An Economic Analysis of Fertility,'" in *Demographic and Economic Change in Developed Countries* (Cambridge, MA: National Bureau of Economic Research, 1960), 233.

19.   Bryan Caplan, "Persuasion, Slack, and Traps: How Can Economists Change the World?" *Public Choice* 142, no. 1–2 (2010): 1–8.

20.   Blinder, *Central Banking*, 59.

Chapter 4

1.   Alan Blinder, "Is Government Too Political?" *Foreign Affairs* 76, no. 6 (1997): 117.

2.   Blinder, "Is Government Too Political?" 117.

3.   Ezra Klein, "The Supreme Court vs. Democracy," *Vox.com*, July 9, 2018.

4.   Richard Neely, *The Product Liability Mess: How Business Can Be Rescued from State Court Politics* (New York: Free Press, 1988), 4. I also recommend another insightful, often whimsical, book by the same author: Richard Neely, *How Courts Govern America* (New Haven: Yale University Press, 1983).

5.   Alexander Tabarrok and Eric Helland, "Court Politics: The Political Economy of Tort Awards," *Journal of Law and Economics* 42, no. 1 (1999): 157–188. Also see Eric Helland and Alexander Tabarrok, "The Effect of Electoral Institutions on Tort Awards," *American Law and Economics Review* 4, no. 2 (2002): 341–370.

6. Elliott Ash and W. Bentley MacLeod, "The Performance of Elected Officials: Evidence from State Supreme Courts," NBER working paper 22071 (2016), 1.

7. John Haley, "The Japanese Judiciary: Maintaining Integrity, Autonomy and the Public Trust," in *Law in Japan: A Turning Point*, ed. Daniel J. Foote (Seattle: University of Washington Press, 2007), 102–103.

8. Courts and Tribunals Judiciary, "Judicial Appointments," accessed August 20, 2018, https://www.judiciary.uk/about-the-judiciary /the-judiciary-the-government-and-the-constitution/jud-acc-ind /jud-appts/.

9. Jimmy Carter, *Why Not the Best? The First 50 Years* (Fayetteville: University of Arkansas Press, 1975).

10. Ash and McLeod, "Performance of Elected Officials," 3.

11. Ash and McLeod, "Performance of Elected Officials," 3.

12. Rafael La Porta, Florencio Lopez-de-Silanes, Cristian Pop-Eleches, and Andrei Shleifer, "Judicial Checks and Balances," *Journal of Political Economy* 112, no. 2 (2004): 445–470.

13. La Porta et al., "Judicial Checks," 457.

14. Michael Baldassare, "The Orange County Bankruptcy: Who's Next?" Public Policy Institute of California research brief (April 1998).

15. Whalley, "Elected versus Appointed," n. 7.

16. Dwight D. Eisenhower, "Farewell Address," (1961), accessed May 23, 2019, https://www.eisenhower.archives.gov/all_about_ike /speeches/farewell_address.pdf.

17. Timothy Besley and Stephen Coate. "Elected Versus Appointed Regulators: Theory and Evidence," *Journal of the European Economic Association* 1, no. 5 (2003): 1176–1206. The longer working paper is even more useful: Timothy Besley and Stephen Coate, "Elected Versus Appointed Regulators: Theory and Evidence," *NBER Working Paper 7579* (2000). Also see Guy L. F. Holburn and Pablo T. Spiller, "Interest Group Representation in Administrative Institutions: The Impact of Consumer Advocates and Elected Commissioners on Regulatory Policy in the United States," working paper (2002).

18. Dino Falaschetti, "Electoral Accountability and Consumer Monopsonists: Evidence from Elected vs. Appointed Regulators," working paper (2007).

19. Falaschetti, "Electoral Accountability," 4.

20. Besley and Coate, "Elected Versus Appointed," 1178.

21. Friedrich August Hayek, "The Use of Knowledge in Society," *American Economic Review* 35, no. 4 (1945): 526.

22. Geoff Edwards and Leonard Waverman, "The Effects of Public Ownership and Regulatory Independence on Regulatory Outcomes," *Journal of Regulatory Economics* 29, no. 1 (2006): 23–67.

23. Edwards and Waverman, "Effects of Public Ownership," 37.

24. Warrick Smith, "Utility Regulators: The Independence Debate," *Public Policy for the Private Sector* 127, no. 1 (1997): 1–4.

25. Lisa Schultz Bressman and Robert B. Thompson, "The Future of Agency Independence," *Vanderbilt Law Review* 63 (2010): 611.

26. Alan S. Blinder, *Advice and Dissent: Why America Suffers When Economics and Politics Collide* (New York: Basic Books, 2018), 9.

27. Blinder, *Advice and Dissent*, 285.

28. Blinder, *Advice and Dissent*, 296.

29. Blinder, *Advice and Dissent*, 296.

30. Blinder, *Advice and Dissent*, 297.

31. Blinder, *Advice and Dissent* 297.

32. Blinder, *Advice and Dissent*, 298.

Chapter 5

1. American Convention on Human Rights, accessed May 23, 2019, https://en.wikisource.org/wiki/American_Convention_on_Human_Rights.

2. United Nations Office of the High Commissioner on Human Rights, "United Nations Guide for Minorities. Pamphlet No. 5: Protection of Minority Rights in the Inter-American Human Rights System," accessed October 29, 2018, https://www.ohchr.org/en/issues/minorities/pages/minoritiesguide.aspx.

3. Koji Maeda and Kaori H. Okano, "Connecting Indigenous Ainu, University and Local Industry in Japan: The Urespa Project," *International Education Journal: Comparative Perspectives* 12, no. 1 (2013): 45–60.

4. Steve Strand, "Ethnicity, Deprivation and Educational Achievement at Age 16 in England: Trends over Time," Department for Education research report (2015).

5. National Center for Education Statistics, "Public High School

Graduation Rates," U.S. Department of Education(May 2018), https://nces.ed.gov/programs/coe/indicator_coi.asp.

6.   Chiefs Assembly on Education, "Information Package," Assembly of First Nations (October 2012), http://www.treatysix.org/pdf/AFN%20Education%20Assembly%20Information%20Package_ENG.pdf.

7.   Vincenzo Memoli, "How Does Political Knowledge Shape Support for Democracy? Some Research Based on the Italian Case," *Bulletin of Italian Politics* 3, no. 1 (2011): 79–102.

8.   Jan-Willem van Prooijen, "Why Education Predicts Decreased Belief in Conspiracy Theories," *Applied Cognitive Psychology* 31, no. 1 (2017): 50–58.

9.   Bryan Caplan, *The Myth of the Rational Voter: Why Democracies Choose Bad Policies* (Princeton: Princeton University Press, 2011).

10.   Alan Blinder, *Advice and Dissent: Central Banking in Theory and Practice* (Cambridge, MA: MIT Press, 1999), 255.

11.   European Union Agency for Fundamental Rights, "The Rights of People with Mental Health Problems and Intellectual Disabilities to Take Part in Politics" (November 2010), http://fra.europa.eu/sites/default/files/fra_report_on_right_to_vote_as_easy_to_read.pdf.

12.   James R. Hansen, *First Man: The Life of Neil A. Armstrong* (New York: Simon and Schuster, 2012).

13.   Jason Brennan, *Against Democracy: New Preface* (Princeton: Princeton University Press, 2017).

14.   Jody Heymann, Adèle Cassola, Amy Raub, and Lipi Mishra, "Constitutional Rights to Health, Public Health and Medical Care: The Status of Health Protections in 191 Countries," *Global Public Health* 8, no. 6 (2013): 644.

15.   Matthias Doepke, Michele Tertilt, and Alessandra Voena, "The Economics and Politics of Women's Rights," *Annual Reviews of Economics* 4, no. 1 (2012): 339–372.

16.   Alan de Bromhead, "Women Voters and Trade Protectionism in the Interwar Years," Oxford Economic Papers 70, no. 1 (2017): 22–46.

17.   Robert A. Heinlein, *Starship Troopers* (New York: Putnam, 1959).

18.   Benjamin Franklin, *Poor Richard's Almanack* (New York: Barnes & Noble, 2004).

19. Daniel Stockemer and François Rocher, "Age, Political Knowledge and Electoral Turnout: A Case Study of Canada," *Commonwealth and Comparative Politics* 55, no. 1 (2017): 41–62.

20. Giorgio Del Vecchio, "Universal Suffrage and Political Capacity," *Loyola Law Review* 11, no. 1 (1961): 1–7.

21. American Civil Liberties Union, "Out of Step with the World: An Analysis of Felony Disenfranchisement in the U.S. and Other Democracies," ACLU (2006).

22. Caroline Wolf Harlow, "Education and Correctional Populations: Bureau of Justice Statistics Special Report" (2003).

23. Gordon Tullock, "The Transitional Gains Trap," *Bell Journal of Economics* 6, no. 2 (1975): 671–678.

24. Mark J. Perry, "Chart of the Day: Creative Destruction, the Uber Effect, and the Slow Death of the NYC Taxi Cartel," *Carpe Diem*, March 17, 2018, http://www.aei.org/publication/chart-of-the-day-creative -destruction-the-uber-effect-and-the-slow-death-of-the-nyc-yellow -taxi/.

25. American Medical Association. "AMA Code of Medical Ethics: Treating Self or Family," accessed October 29, 2018, https://www.ama-assn.org/delivering-care/treating-self-or-family.

26. Robert Anson Heinlein, *Expanded Universe: The New Worlds of Robert A. Heinlein* (New York: Grosset & Dunlap, 1980).

Chapter 6

1. Alexander Hamilton to Robert Morris, April 30, 1781, U.S. National Archives.

2. Marcia Stigum and Anthony Crescenzi, *Stigum's Money Market*, 4th ed. (New York: McGraw-Hill, 2007), 305–307.

3. Ed Christman, "The Whole Story Behind David Bowie's $55 Million Wall Street Trailblaze," *Billboard*, January 13, 2016.

4. Christopher A. Sims, "Paper Money," *American Economic Review* 103, no. 2 (2013): 563–584.

5. There was a 9% nominal rate on the constant maturity Treasury and a 2.6% GDP inflation rate over the next decade.

6. Miwa Murphy, "Ministry Goes Offshore to Diversify Holders of JGBs," *Japan Times*, June 27, 2006.

7. Martin A. Weiss, "The Paris Club and International Debt Relief," Congressional Research Service (Washington, DC: Library of Congress, 2013), 1.

8. Club de Paris, "The Six Principles," accessed May 24, 2019, http://www.clubdeparis.org/en/communications/page/the-six-principles.

9. Alexander Hamilton, *First Report on the Public Credit* (Washington, DC: US Government Printing Office, 1908).

10. Douglass C. North and Barry R. Weingast, "Constitutions and Commitment: The Evolution of Institutions Governing Public Choice in Seventeenth-Century England," *Journal of Economic History* 49, no. 4 (1989): 803–832.

11. Hilton L. Root, "Tying the King's Hands: Credible Commitments and Royal Fiscal Policy During the Old Regime," *Rationality and Society* 1, no. 2 (1989): 240–258.

12. Sebastian Edwards, "Sovereign Default, Debt Restructuring, and Recovery Rates: Was the Argentinean 'Haircut' Excessive?" *Open Economies Review* 26, no. 5 (2015): 839–867.

13. Thomas Friedman, "Don't Mess with Moody's," *New York Times*, February 22, 1995.

Chapter 7

1. William L. Riordan, *Plunkitt of Tammany Hall: A Series of Very Plain Talks on Very Practical Politics* (New York: Penguin, 1995), 3.

2. Riordan, *Tammany Hall*, 6.

3. Riordan, *Tammany Hall*, 24.

4. Carol Hanisch, "The Personal Is Political," in *Notes from the Second Year: Women's Liberation*, ed. Shulamith Firestone (New York: Shulamith Firestone, 1970).

5. Riordan, *Tammany Hall*, 25.

6. *Merriam-Webster's Collegiate Dictionary*, 11th ed. (New York: Merriam-Webster, 2014).

7. Donald A. Wittman, *The Myth of Democratic Failure: Why Political Institutions Are Efficient* (Chicago: University of Chicago Press, 1995).

8. Donald Wittman, "Why Democracies Produce Efficient Results," *Journal of Political Economy* 97, no. 6 (1989): 1395–1424.

9. Tyler Cowen, "The Wisdom of Garett Jones, a Continuing Series,"

Marginal Revolution, January 26, 2010, https://marginalrevolution.com/marginalrevolution/2010/01/the-wisdom-of-garett-jones-a-continuing-series.html.

10. Tyler Cowen, "Congress Needs to Bring Back Earmarks," *Bloomberg Opinion*, January 9, 2018.

11. Cowen, "Congress Needs to Bring Back Earmarks."

12. Rauch, *Political Realism*, 7.

13. Rauch, *Political Realism*, 11.

14. Rauch, *Political Realism*, 11.

15. Martin Gurri, *The Revolt of the Public and the Crisis of Authority in the New Millennium* (San Francisco: Stripe Press, 2018.

16. Christopher Nolan, *The Dark Knight Trilogy* (London: Faber & Faber, 2012).

Chapter 8

1. European Parliament, "Exploratory Study: Major Trends in European Public Opinion with Regard to the European Union," Directorate-General for Communication, updated November 2015, http://www.europarl.europa.eu/pdf/eurobarometre/2015/major_change/eb_historical_deskresearch_en.pdf. Also see European Commission, "Eurobarometer 69: 4. The European Union and Its Citizens," Directorate-General for Communication. November 2008, http://ec.europa.eu/commfrontoffice/publicopinion/archives/eb/eb69/eb69_part2_en.pdfl.

2. Andrew Moravcsik, "Reassessing Legitimacy in the European Union," *Journal of Common Market Studies* 40, no. 4 (2002): 603–624.

3. Morten Egeberg, Åse Gornitzka, and Jarle Trondal, "A Not So Technocratic Executive? Everyday Interaction Between the European Parliament and the Commission," *West European Politics* 37, no. 1 (2014): 1–18.

4. Agnieszka Walczak and Wouter van der Brug, "The Quality of Representation in European Elections," in *Proceedings of the 6th ECPR General Conference*, University of Iceland, 2011, 25–27.

5. Ryan Heath, "Europeans Love the EU (and Populists too)," *Politico*, May 23, 2018, https://www.politico.eu/article/europeans-love-the-eu-and-populists-too/.

6. Charlie Dunmore, "EU Finds Time to Tell Restaurants How to Serve Olive Oil," *Reuters*, May 18, 2013.

7. Joshua C. Hall, Robert A. Lawson, and Rachael Wogsland, "The European Union and Economic Freedom," *Global Economy Journal* 11, no. 3 (2011): 1850232. Also see Danko Tarabar and Andrew T. Young. "Liberalizing Reforms and the European Union: Accession, Membership, and Convergence," *Southern Economic Journal* 83, no. 4 (2017): 932–951.

8. Robert D. Putnam, "E Pluribus Unum: Diversity and Community in the Twenty?First Century: The 2006 Johan Skytte Prize Lecture," *Scandinavian Political Studies* 30, no. 2 (2007): 137–174.

9. Edward L. Glaeser, David I. Laibson, Jose A. Scheinkman, and Christine L. Soutter, "Measuring Trust," *Quarterly Journal of Economics* 115, no. 3 (2000): 811–846.

10. Jonas Hjort, "Ethnic Divisions and Production in Firms," *Quarterly Journal of Economics* 129, no. 4 (2014): 1899–1946.

11. Patrick Joseph O'Brien, *Will Rogers, Ambassador of Good Will, Prince of Wit and Wisdom* (John C. Winston, 1935).

12. W. J. Wagner, "May 3, 1791, and the Polish Constitutional Tradition," *Polish Review* 36, no. 4 (1991): 383–395.

13. Knut Wicksell, *Finanztheoretische Untersuchungen: Nebst Darstellung und Kritik des Steuerwesens Schwedens* (G. Fischer, 1896).

14. James M. Buchanan and Gordon Tullock, *The Calculus of Consent* (Ann Arbor: University of Michigan Press, 1962).

15. Buchanan and Tullock, *Calculus*, 85.

16. Buchanan and Tullock, *Calculus*, 89.

17. Buchanan and Tullock, *Calculus*, 96.

18. Robert A. Mundell, "A Theory of Optimum Currency Areas," *American Economic Review* 51, no. 4 (1961): 657–665.

19. Matthew Yglesias, "The Eurozone Is a Political Project, Not an Economic One," *Vox*, July 6, 2015.

20. Phillip Connor, "The Most Common Mediterranean Migration Paths to European Have Changed Since 2009," *FactTank: News in the Numbers*, Pew Research Center, September 18, 2018. http://www.pewresearch.org/fact-tank/2018/09/18/the-most-common-mediterranean-migration-paths-into-europe-have-changed-since-2009/.

21. Jacopo Barigazzi and Maïa de la Baume, "EU Forces Through Refugee Deal," *Politic*, September 21, 2015. See also European Commission, "Relocation and Resettlement: EU Member States Urgently Need to Deliver," press release, Brussels, March 16, 2016.

22. Eric Maurice, "EU Buries Migration Dispute for Now," *EU Observer*, October 20, 2016, https://euobserver.com/migration/135576.

23. Nikolaj Nielsen and Eszter Zalan, "Salzburg Summit Presses for Bigger Frontex Mandate," *EU Observe*, September 21, 2018, https://euobserver.com/migration/142917.

24. Dyfed Loesche, "Refugee Arrivals in the Mediterranean in Perspective," *Statista*, July 19, 2017, https://www.statista.com/chart/10327/migrant-sea-arrivals-across-the-mediterranean/.

25. Mark Akkerman, "Europe's Solution to Migration Is to Outsource It To Africa," *EU Observer*, May 10, 2018, https://euobserver.com/opinion/141784.

Chapter 9

1. Lant Pritchett and Michael Woolcock, "Solutions When the Solution Is the Problem: Arraying the Disarray in Development," *World Development* 32, no. 2 (2004): 204.

2. Pritchett and Woolcock, "Solutions," 192.

3. Pritchett and Woolcock, "Solutions," 192.

4. Monty G. Marshall, Ted Gurr, and Keith Jaggers, "Center for Systemic Peace: Polity IV Country Report 2010: Singapore," *Polity IV Project*, 2011, http://www.systemicpeace.org/polity/Singapore2010.pdf.

5. Economist Intelligence Unit, *Democracy Index 2018: Me Too? Political Participation, Protest and Democracy* (London: Economist, 2018), 11.

6. Lee Kuan Yew, *The Wit and Wisdom of Lee Kuan Yew* (Paris: Editions Didier Millet, 2013), Kindle.

7. Lee, *Wit and Wisdom*.

8. Lee, *Wit and Wisdom*.

9. William F. Case, "Can the 'Halfway House' Stand? Semidemocracy and Elite Theory in Three Southeast Asian Countries," *Comparative Politics* 28, no. 4 (1996): 437–464.

10. Case, *Semidemocracy*, 443.

11. Purely hypothetical: I have great neighbors.

Conclusion

1. Aristotle, *Aristotle's Politics and Athenian Constitution*, trans. John Warrington (New York: Dutton, 1959), book IV, sec. 1295.

2. Aristotle, *Aristotle's Politics*, book IV, sec. 1295.

3. Aristotle, *Aristotle's Politics*, book IV, sec. 1296.

4. Aristotle, *Aristotle's Politics*, book IV, sec. 1293.

5. Aristotle, *Aristotle's Politics*, book IV, sec. 1294.

6. Aristotle, *Aristotle's Politics*, book IV, sec. 1295.

7. Polybius, *The Histories*, in *The Portable Greek Historians: The Essence of Herodotus, Thucydides, Xenophon, Polybius*, ed. Moses I. Finley (New York: Penguin, 1977), book VI, para. 3.

8. Polybius, *The Histories*, book VI, para. 3.

9. Peter Bondanela and Mark Musa, *The Portable Machiavelli* (New York: Penguin Books, 1979), book 1, chap. 2, 179.

10. Bondanela and Musa, *The Portable Machiavelli*, book 1, chap. 2, 179.

11. Robert A. Dahl, *Who Governs? Democracy and Power in an American City* (New Haven: Yale University Press, 2005).

12. Robert A. Dahl, *On Democracy* (New Haven: Yale University Press, 2008).

13. Carveth Read, *Logic, Deductive and Inductive* (A. Moring, 1909).

Bibliography

Acemoglu, Daron, Suresh Naidu, Pascual Restrepo, and James A. Robinson. "Democracy Does Cause Growth." *Journal of Political Economy* 127, no. 1 (2019): 47–100.

Akkerman, Mark. "Europe's Solution to Migration Is to Outsource It to Africa." *EU Observer*, May 10, 2018. https://euobserver.com/opinion/141784.

Alemán, Eduardo, and Ernesto Calvo. "Analyzing Legislative Success in Latin America: The Case of Democratic Argentina." In *The Study of New Democracies in Latin America*. Edited by Guillermo O'Donnell, Joseph Tulchin, and Augusto Varas, with Adam Stubits. Washington, DC: Woodrow Wilson International Center for Scholars, 2008.

Alesina, Alberto, and Andrea Stella. "The Politics of Monetary Policy." In *Handbook of Monetary Economics*, vol. 3, edited by Benjamin Friedman and Michael Woodford, pp. 1001–105. Amsterdam: North-Holland, 2010.

Alesina, Alberto, and Lawrence H. Summers. "Central Bank Independence and Macroeconomic Performance: Some Comparative Evidence." *Journal of Money, Credit and Banking* 25, no. 2 (1993): 151–162.

Almond, Gabriel Abraham, and Sidney Verba. *The Civic Culture: Political Attitudes and Democracy in Five Nations*. Princeton: Princeton University Press, 2015.

American Civil Liberties Union. "Out of Step with the World: An Analysis of Felony Disenfranchisement in the U.S. and other Democracies." ACLU, 2006.

American Convention on Human Rights. Accessed May 23, 2019, https://en.wikisource.org/wiki/American_Convention_on_Human_Rights.

American Medical Association. "AMA Code of Medical Ethics: Treating Self or Family." Accessed October 29, 2018, https://www.ama-assn.org/delivering-care/treating-self-or-family.

Aristotle. *Aristotle's Politics and Athenian Constitution*. Translated by John Warrington. New York: Dutton, 1959.

Ash, Elliott, and W. Bentley MacLeod. "The Performance of Elected Officials: Evidence from State Supreme Courts." NBER working paper 22071, 2016.

Baldassare, Michael. "The Orange County Bankruptcy: Who's Next?" Public Policy Institute of California research brief. April 1998.

Barigazzi, Jacopo, and Maïa de la Baume, "EU Forces Through Refugee Deal." *Politico*, September 21, 2015.

Barro, Robert J. "Democracy and Growth." *Journal of Economic Growth* 1, no. 1 (1996): 1–27.

———. "Inflation and Economic Growth," *Annals of Economics and Finance* 14, no. 1 (2013): 121–144.

Bastiat, Frédéric. "What Is Seen and What Is Not Seen." *Ideas on Liberty* 51 (2001): 12–16.

Baumgartner, Frank R., Sylvain Brouard, Emiliano Grossman, Sebastien G. Lazardeux, and Jonathan Moody. "Divided Government, Legislative Productivity, and Policy Change in the USA and France." *Governance* 27, no. 3 (2014): 423–447.

Beckman, Ludvig. *The Frontiers of Democracy: The Right to Vote and Its Limits*. Berlin: Springer, 2009.

Bell, Mark S., and Kai Quek. "Authoritarian Public Opinion and the Democratic Peace." *International Organization* 72, no. 1 (2018): 227–242.

Besley, Timothy, and Stephen Coate. "Elected Versus Appointed Regulators: Theory and Evidence." NBER working paper 7579, 2000.

———. "Elected Versus Appointed Regulators: Theory and Evidence." *Journal of the European Economic Association* 1, no. 5 (2003): 1176–1206.

Blanes i Vidal, Jordi, Mirko Draca, and Christian Fons-Rosen, "Revolving Door Lobbyists." *American Economic Review* 102, no. 7 (2012): 3731–3748.

Blinder, Alan S. *Advice and Dissent: Why America Suffers When Economics and Politics Collide.* New York: Basic Books, 2018.

———. *Central Banking in Theory and Practice.* Cambridge, MA: MIT Press, 1999.

———. "Is Government Too Political?" *Foreign Affairs* 76. no. 6 (1997): 115–126.

Bondonela, Peter, and Mark Musa. *The Portable Machiavelli.* New York: Penguin Books, 1979.

Brennan, Jason. *Against Democracy: New Preface.* Princeton: Princeton University Press, 2017.

Bressman, Lisa Schultz, and Robert B. Thompson. "The Future of Agency Independence." *Vanderbilt Law Review* 63 (2010): 599–672.

Buchanan, James M., and Gordon Tullock. *The Calculus of Consent.* Ann Arbor: University of Michigan Press, 1962.

Caplan, Bryan. "Persuasion, Slack, and Traps: How Can Economists Change the World?" *Public Choice* 142, no. 1–2 (2010): 1–8.

———. *The Myth of the Rational Voter: Why Democracies Choose Bad Policies.* Princeton: Princeton University Press, 2011.

Card, Orson Scott. *Ender's Game.* New York: Tor Books, 1985.

Carter, Jimmy. *Why Not the Best? The First 50 Years.* Fayetteville: University of Arkansas Press, 1975.

Case, William F. "Can the 'Halfway House' Stand? Semidemocracy and Elite Theory in Three Southeast Asian Countries." *Comparative Politics* 28, no. 4 (1996): 437–464.

Chiefs Assembly on Education. "Information Package." Assembly of First Nations, October 2012. http://www.treatysix.org/pdf/AFN%20 Education%20Assembly%20Information%20Package_ENG.pdf.

Club de Paris, "The Six Principles." Accessed May 24, 2019, http://www .clubdeparis.org/en/communications/page/the-six-principles.

Conconi, Paola, David R. DeRemer, Georg Kirchsteiger, Lorenzo Trimarchi, and Maurizio Zanardi. "Suspiciously Timed Trade Disputes." *Journal of International Economics* 105 (2017): 57–76.

Conconi, Paola, Giovanni Facchini, and Maurizio Zanardi. "Policymakers'

Horizon and Trade Reforms: The Protectionist Effect of Elections." *Journal of International Economics* 94, no. 1 (2014): 102–118.

Connor, Phillip. "The Most Common Mediterranean Migration Paths to Europe Have Changed Since 2009." *FactTank: News in the Numbers.* Pew Research Center, September 18, 2018. http://www.pewresearch .org/fact-tank/2018/09/18/the-most-common-mediterranean -migration-paths-into-europe-have-changed-since-2009/.

Cowen, Tyler. "Congress Needs to Bring Back Earmarks." *Bloomberg Opinion*, January 9, 2018.

———. "The Wisdom of Garett Jones, a Continuing Series," *Marginal Revolution*, January 26, 2010. https://marginalrevolution.com/marginal-revolution/2010/01/the-wisdom-of-garett-jones-a-continuing-series .html.

Cukierman, Alex. "Central Bank Independence and Policy Results: Theory and Evidence." Lecture prepared for the international conference on Stability and Economic Growth: The Role of the Central Bank, Mexico City, 2005.

———. *Central Bank Strategy, Credibility, and Independence: Theory and Evidence.* Cambridge, MA: MIT Press, 1992.

Dahl, Robert A. *On Democracy.* New Haven: Yale University Press, 1998.

Dal Bó, Ernesto, and Martín A. Rossi. "Term Length and the Effort of Politicians." *Review of Economic Studies* 78, no. 4 (2011): 1237–1263.

Daley, Matthew F., Lori A. Crane, Lauri E. Markowitz, Sandra R. Black, Brenda L. Beaty, Jennifer Barrow, Christine Babbel et al. "Human Papillomavirus Vaccination Practices: Survey of US Physicians 18 Months After Licensure." *Pediatrics* 126, no. 3 (2010): 425 –433.

Daley, Matthew F., Nicole Liddon, Lori A. Crane, Brenda L. Beaty, Jennifer Barrow, Christine Babbel, Lauri E. Markowitz et al. "A National Survey of Pediatrician Knowledge and Attitudes Regarding Human Papillomavirus Vaccination." *Pediatrics* 118, no. 6 (2006): 2280–2289.

de Bromhead, Alan. "Women Voters and Trade Protectionism in the Interwar Years." *Oxford Economic Papers* 70, no. 1 (2017): 22–46.

Del Vecchio, Giorgio. "Universal Suffrage and Political Capacity." *Loyola Law Review* 11, no. 1 (1961): 1–7.

Di Tella, Rafael, Robert J. MacCulloch, and Andrew Oswald. "Preferences over Inflation and Unemployment: Evidence from Surveys of Happiness." *American Economic Review* 91, no. 1 (2001): 335–341.

Doepke, Matthias, Michele Tertilt, and Alessandra Voena. "The Economics and Politics of Women's Rights." *Annual Review of Economics* 4, no. 1 (2012): 339–372.

Donadio, Rachel. "The 'Submission' of Michel Houellebecq: Interview Excerpts." *New York Times*, October 12, 2015.

Duesenberry, James. "Comment on 'An Economic Analysis of Fertility' " In *Demographic and Economic Change in Developed Countries*. Cambridge, MA: National Bureau of Economic Research, 1960.

Dunmore, Charlie. "EU Finds Time to Tell Restaurants How to Serve Olive Oil." Reuters, May 18, 2013.

William Easterly, "National Policies and Economic Growth: A Reappraisal," in *Handbook of Economic Growth*, edited by Philippe Aghion and Steven Durlauf, vol. 1, pp. 1015–1059. New York: Elsevier, 2005.

Easterly, William, Roberta Gatti, and Sergio Kurlat. "Development, Democracy, and Mass Killings." *Journal of Economic Growth* 11, no. 2 (2006): 129–156.

Eberhardt, Markus, and Andrea F. Presbitero. "Public Debt and Growth: Heterogeneity and Non-Linearity." *Journal of International Economics* 97, no. 1 (2015): 45–58.

Economist Intelligence Unit. *Democracy Index* 2018: *Me Too? Political Participation, Protest and Democracy*. London: Economist, 2018.

Edwards, Geoff, and Leonard Waverman. "The Effects of Public Ownership and Regulatory Independence on Regulatory Outcomes." *Journal of Regulatory Economics* 29, no. 1 (2006): 23–67.

Edwards, Sebastian, and Andrea F. Presbitero. "Sovereign Default, Debt Restructuring, and Recovery Rates: Was the Argentinean 'Haircut' Excessive?" *Open Economies Review* 26, no. 5 (2015): 839–867.

Egeberg, Morten, Åse Gornitzka, and Jarle Trondal. "A Not So Technocratic Executive? Everyday Interaction Between the European Parliament and the Commission." *West European Politics* 37, no. 1 (2014): 1–18.

Eisenhower, Dwight D. "Farewell Address." 1961. https://www.eisenhower.archives.gov/all_about_ike/speeches/farewell_address.pdf.

European Union Agency for Fundamental Rights. "The Rights of People with Mental Health Problems and Intellectual Disabilities to Take Part in Politics." November 2010. http://fra.europa.eu/sites/default/files/fra_report_on_right_to_vote_as_easy_to_read.pdf.

European Commission. "Eurobarometer 69: 4. The European Union and Its Citizens." Directorate-General for Communication. November 2008. http://ec.europa.eu/commfrontoffice/publicopinion/archives/eb/eb69/eb69_part2_en.pdf.

European Commission. "Relocation and Resettlement: EU Member States Urgently Need to Deliver." Press release, Brussels, March 16, 2016.

European Parliament. "Exploratory Study: Major Trends in European Public Opinion with Regard to the European Union." Directorate-General for Communication, November 2015. http://www.europarl.europa.eu/pdf/eurobarometre/2015/major_change/eb_historical_deskresearch_en.pdf.

Fair, Ray C. "Presidential and Congressional Vote?Share Equations." *American Journal of Political Science* 53, no. 1 (2009): 55–72.

Falaschetti, Dino. "Electoral Accountability and Consumer Monopsonists: Evidence from Elected vs. Appointed Regulators." Working paper, 2007.

Franklin, Benjamin. *Poor Richard's Almanack*. New York: Barnes & Noble, 2004.

Frieden, Jeffry, Piero Ghezzi, and Ernesto Stein. "Politics and Exchange Rates: A Cross-Country Approach to Latin America." In *The Currency Game: Exchange Rate Politics in Latin America*. Edited by Jeffry Frieden and Ernesto Stein. Baltimore, MD: Johns Hopkins University Press, 2001.

Friedman, Thomas "Don't Mess with Moody's." *New York Times*, February 22, 1995.

Gerring, John, Philip Bond, William T. Barndt, and Carola Moreno. "Democracy and Economic Growth: A Historical Perspective." *World Politics* 57, no. 3 (2005): 323–364.

Glaeser, Edward L., David I. Laibson, Jose A. Scheinkman, and Christine L. Soutter. "Measuring Trust." *Quarterly Journal of Economics* 115, no. 3 (2000): 811–846.

Grilli, Vittorio, Donato Masciandaro, and Guido Tabellini. "Political and Monetary Institutions and Public Financial Policies in the Industrial Countries." *Economic Policy* 6, no. 13 (1991): 341–392.

Gurri, Martin. *The Revolt of the Public and the Crisis of Authority in the New Millennium*. San Francisco: Stripe Press, 2018.

Haley, John. "The Japanese Judiciary: Maintaining Integrity, Autonomy and the Public Trust." In *Law in Japan: A Turning Point*. Edited by Daniel J. Foote. Seattle: University of Washington Press, 2007.

Hall, Joshua C., Robert A. Lawson, and Rachael Wogsland. "The European Union and Economic Freedom." *Global Economy Journal* 11, no. 3 (2011): 1850232.

Hamilton, Alexander. *First Report on the Public Credit*. Washington, DC: U.S. Government Printing Office, 1908.

———. Letter to Robert Morris, April 30, 1781. U.S. National Archives.

Hanisch, Carol. "The Personal Is Political." In *Notes from the Second Year: Women's Liberation*. New York: Shulamith Firestone, 1970.

Hansen, James R. *First Man: The Life of Neil A. Armstrong*. New York: Simon and Schuster, 2012.

Harlow, Caroline Wolf. "Education and Correctional Populations." Bureau of Justice Statistics special report. 2003.

Hayek, Friedrich August. "The Use of Knowledge in Society." *American Economic Review* 35, no. 4 (1945): 519–530.

Heath, Ryan. "Europeans Love the EU (and Populists Too)." *Politico*. May 23, 2018. https://www.politico.eu/article/europeans-love-the-eu-and-populists-too/.

Hegre, Håvard. "Democracy and Armed Conflict." *Journal of Peace Research* 51, no. 2 (2014): 159.

Hegre, Håvard, Michael Bernhard, and Jan Teorell. "Reassessing the Democratic Peace: A Novel Test Based on the Varieties of Democracy Data." Working paper, 2018.

Heinlein, Robert Anson. *Expanded Universe: The New Worlds of Robert A. Heinlein*. New York: Grosset & Dunlap, 1980.

———. *Starship Troopers*. New York: Putnam, 1959.

Helland, Eric, and Alexander Tabarrok. "The Effect of Electoral Institutions on Tort Awards." *American Law and Economics Review* 4, no. 2 (2002): 341–370.

Heymann, Jody, Adèle Cassola, Amy Raub, and Lipi Mishra. "Constitutional Rights to Health, Public Health and Medical Care: The Status of Health Protections in 191 Countries." *Global Public Health* 8, no. 6 (2013): 639–653.

Hirschman, Albert O. *The Passions and the Interests: Political Arguments for Capitalism Before Its Triumph.* Princeton: Princeton University Press, 1977.

Hjort, Jonas. "Ethnic Divisions and Production in Firms." *Quarterly Journal of Economics* 129, no. 4 (2014): 1899–1946.

Holburn, Guy L. F., and Pablo T. Spiller. "Interest Group Representation in Administrative Institutions: The Impact of Consumer Advocates and Elected Commissioners on Regulatory Policy in the United States." Working paper, 2002.

Initiative on Global Markets Forum. "France's Labor Market." May 17, 2017.

———. "Trade Within Europe." December 7, 2016.

———. "China-Europe Trade." April 12, 2018.

Jones, Benjamin F., and Benjamin A. Olken. "Do Leaders Matter? National Leadership and Growth Since World War II." *Quarterly Journal of Economics* 120, no. 3 (2005): 835–864.

Klein, Ezra. "The Supreme Court vs. Democracy." *Vox.com*, July 9, 2018.

Kleine, Mareike, and Clement Minaudier. "Negotiating Under Political Uncertainty: National Elections and the Dynamics of International Co-operation." *British Journal of Political Science* 49, no. 1 (2017): 315–337.

Klomp, Jeroen, and Jakob De Haan. "Central Bank Independence and Financial Instability." *Journal of Financial Stability* 5, no. 4 (2009): 321–338.

Kydland, Finn E., and Edward C. Prescott. "Time to Build and Aggregate Fluctuations." *Econometrica* (1982): 1345–1370.

La Porta, Rafael, Florencio Lopez-de-Silanes, Cristian Pop-Eleches, and Andrei Shleifer. "Judicial Checks and Balances." *Journal of Political Economy* 112, no. 2 (2004): 445–470.

Lee Kuan Yew. *The Wit and Wisdom of Lee Kuan Yew.* Singapore: Editions Didier Millet, 2013.

Liow, Lee Hsiang, Mikael Fortelius, Ella Bingham, Kari Lintulaakso, Heikki Mannila, Larry Flynn, and Nils Chr. Stenseth. "Higher Origination and Extinction Rates in Larger Mammals." *Proceedings of the National Academy of Sciences* 105, no. 16 (2008): 6097–6102.

Lipset, Seymour Martin. "Some Social Requisites of Democracy: Economic Development and Political Legitimacy." *American Political Science Review* 53, no. 1 (1959): 69–105.

Long Jr., John B., and Charles I. Plosser. "Real Business Cycles." *Journal of Political Economy* 91, no. 1 (1983): 39–69.

Machiavelli, Niccolò. *The Discourses.*

Maeda, Koji, and Kaori H. Okano. "Connecting Indigenous Ainu, University and Local Industry in Japan: The Urespa Project." *International Education Journal: Comparative Perspectives* 12, no. 1 (2013): 45–60.

Mankiw, Gregory N. *Principles of Macroeconomics*, 8th ed. Boston: Cengage, 2018.

Marshall, Monty G., and Ted Robert Gurr. *Polity IV Project: Political Regime Characteristics and Transitions*, 1800–2016. *Dataset Users' Manual*. Vienna, VA: Center for Systemic Peace. 2017.

Marshall, Monty G., Ted Gurr, and Keith Jaggers. "Center for Systemic Peace: Polity IV Country Report 2010; Singapore." Vienna, VA: Center for Systemic Peace, 2011. http://www.systemicpeace.org/polity/Singapore2010.pdf

Maskin, Eric, and Jean Tirole. "The Politician and the Judge: Accountability in Government." *American Economic Review* 94, no. 4 (2004): 1034–1054.

Maurice, Eric. "EU Buries Migration Dispute for Now." *EU Observer*, October 20, 2016. https://euobserver.com/migration/135576.

Mayhew, David R. *Congress: The Electoral Connection*. New Haven: Yale University Press, 1974.

Memoli, Vincenzo. "How Does Political Knowledge Shape Support for Democracy? Some Research Based on the Italian Case." *Bulletin of Italian Politics* 3, no. 1 (2011): 79–102.

Merriam-Webster's Collegiate Dictionary, 11th ed. New York: Merriam-Webster, 2014.

Moravcsik, Andrew. "Reassessing Legitimacy in the European Union." *Journal of Common Market Studies* 40, no. 4 (2002): 603–624.

Mundell, Robert A. "A Theory of Optimum Currency Areas." *American Economic Review* 51, no. 4 (1961): 657–665.

Murphy, Miwa. "Ministry Goes Offshore to Diversify Holders of JGBs." *Japan Times*, June 27, 2006.

National Center for Education Statistics. "Public High School Graduation Rates." Washington, DC: U.S. Department of Education, May 2018. https://nces.ed.gov/programs/coe/indicator_coi.asp.

Neely, Richard. *How Courts Govern America*. New Haven: Yale University Press, 1983.

———. *The Product Liability Mess: How Business Can Be Rescued from State Court Politics*. New York: Free Press, 1988.

Nielsen, Nikolaj and Eszter Zalan. "Salzburg Summit Presses for Bigger Frontex Mandate." *EU Observer*, September 21, 2018. https://euobserver.com/migration/142917

Nolan, Christopher. *The Dark Knight Trilogy*. London: Faber & Faber, 2012.

North, Douglass C., and Barry R. Weingast. "Constitutions and Commitment: The Evolution of Institutions Governing Public Choice in Seventeenth-Century England." *Journal of Economic History* 49, no. 4 (1989): 803–832.

Norton, Ben. "Koch-Funded Economist Wants 'Less Democracy.'" *Counterpunch.org*, March 27, 2015. https://www.counterpunch.org/2015/03/27/koch-funded-economist-wants-less-democracy/.

O'Brien, Patrick Joseph. *Will Rogers, Ambassador of Good Will, Prince of Wit and Wisdom*. Philadelphia: John C. Winston, 1935.

Oneal, John R., and Bruce Russett. "Assessing the Liberal Peace with Alternative Specifications: Trade Still Reduces Conflict." *Journal of Peace Research* 36, no. 4 (1999): 423–442.

Perry, Mark J. "Chart of the Day: Creative Destruction, the Uber Effect, and the Slow Death of the NYC Taxi Cartel." *Carpe Diem*, March 17, 2018. http://www.aei.org/publication/chart-of-the-day-creative-destruction-the-uber-effect-and-the-slow-death-of-the-nyc-yellow-taxi/.

Polybius. *The Histories*, in *The Portable Greek Historians: The Essence of Herodotus, Thucydides, Xenophon, Polybius*, edited by Moses I. Finley, book VI, para. 3 . New York: Penguin, 1977.

Posso, Alberto, and George B. Tawadros. "Does Greater Central Bank Independence Really Lead to Lower Inflation? Evidence from Panel Data." *Economic Modelling* 33 (2013): 244–247.

Pritchett, Lant, and Michael Woolcock. "Solutions When the Solution Is the Problem: Arraying the Disarray in Development." *World Development* 32, no. 2 (2004): 191–212.

Putnam, Robert D. "E Pluribus Unum: Diversity and Community in the Twenty-First Century; The 2006 Johan Skytte Prize Lecture." *Scandinavian Political Studies* 30, no. 2 (2007): 137–174.

Rauch, Jonathan. *Political Realism: How Hacks, Machines, Big Money, and Back-Room Deals Can Strengthen American Democracy*. Washington, DC: Brookings Institution Press, 2015.

Read, Carveth. *Logic, Deductive and Inductive*. A. Moring, 1909.

Rickard, Stephanie J., and Teri L. Caraway. "International Negotiations in the Shadow of National Elections." *International Organization* 68, no. 3 (2014): 701–720.

Riordan, William L. *Plunkitt of Tammany Hall: A Series of Very Plain Talks on Very Practical Politics*. New York: Penguin, 1995.

Rogoff, Kenneth. "The Optimal Degree of Commitment to an Intermediate Monetary Target." *Quarterly Journal of Economics* 100, no. 4 (1985): 1169–1189.

Root, Hilton L. "Tying the King's Hands: Credible Commitments and Royal Fiscal Policy During the Old Regime." *Rationality and Society* 1, no. 2 (1989): 240–258.

Rousseau, Jean-Jacques. "The Social Contract." In *"The Social Contract" and Other Later Political Writings*, 39–152. Cambridge: Cambridge University Press, 1997.

Samuelson, Paul A., and Robert M. Solow. "Analytical Aspects of Anti-Inflation Policy." *American Economic Review Papers and Proceedings* 50(2): 177–194.

Schulhof, Natalie. "'Less Democracy, Better Government,' Says Mason Professor." *Fourth Estate*, March 3, 2015. http://gmufour thestate.com/2015/03/03/less-democracy-better-government-says-mason-professor.

Schelker, Mark. "The Influence of Auditor Term Length and Term Limits on US State General Obligation Bond Ratings." *Public Choice* 150, no. 1–2 (2012): 27–49.

Sen, Amartya K. *Development as Freedom*. New York: Oxford University Press, 2001.

Shepsle, Kenneth A., Robert P. Van Houweling, Samuel J. Abrams, and Peter C. Hanson. "The Senate Electoral Cycle and Bicameral Appropriations Politics." *American Journal of Political Science* 53, no. 2 (2009): 343–359.

Sims, Christopher A. "Paper Money." *American Economic Review* 103, no. 2 (2013): 563–584.

Smith, Warrick. "Utility Regulators: The Independence Debate." *Public Policy for the Private Sector* 127, no. 1 (1997): 1–4.

Stigum, Marcia, and Anthony Crescenzi. *Stigum's Money Market*, 4th ed. New York: McGraw-Hill, 2007.

Stockemer, Daniel, and François Rocher. "Age, Political Knowledge and Electoral Turnout: A Case Study of Canada." *Commonwealth and Comparative Politics* 55, no. 1 (2017): 41–62.

Stolarchuk, Jewel. " 'Buffet-Syndrome' Explanation Is 'Completely at Odds with Reality': SDP Chairman." *Independent* (Singapore), March 15, 2018. http://theindependent.sg/buffet-syndrome-explanation-is -completely-at-odds-with-reality-sdp-chairman/.

Strand, Steve. "Ethnicity, Deprivation and Educational Achievement at Age 16 in England: Trends over Time." Department for Education Research Report, 2015.

Tabarrok, Alexander, and Eric Helland. "Court Politics: The Political Economy of Tort Awards." *Journal of Law and Economics* 42, no. 1 (1999): 157–188.

Tarabar, Danko, and Andrew T. Young. "Liberalizing Reforms and the European Union: Accession, Membership, and Convergence." *Southern Economic Journal* 83, no. 4 (2017): 932–951.

Titiunik, Rocio. "Drawing Your Senator from a Jar: Term Length and Legislative Behavior." *Political Science Research and Methods* 4, no. 2 (2016): 293–316.

Tobin, James, "On Improving the Economic Status of the Negro." In *The Negro American*, edited by Talcott Parsons and Kenneth Bancroft Clark. Boston: Houghton Mifflin, 1966.

Tullock, Gordon. "The Transitional Gains Trap." *Bell Journal of Economics* 6, no. 2 (1975): 671–678.

U.K. Courts and Tribunals Judiciary. "Judicial Appointments." Accessed August 20, 2018, https://www.judiciary.uk/about-the-judiciary /the-judiciary-the-government-and-the-constitution/jud-acc-ind /jud-appts/.

United Nations Office of the High Commissioner on Human Rights. "United Nations Guide for Minorities. Pamphlet No. 5: Protection of Minority Rights in the Inter-American Human Rights System." Accessed October 29, 2018, https://www.ohchr.org/en/issues/minorities/pages/minoritiesguide.aspx.

United Nations Women Watch. *Women and Elections: Guide to Promoting the Participation of Women in Elections.* New York: United Nations, 2005. http://www.un.org/womenwatch/osagi/wps/publication/Chapter4.htm.

van Prooijen, Jan?Willem. "Why Education Predicts Decreased Belief in Conspiracy Theories." *Applied Cognitive Psychology* 31, no. 1 (2017): 50–58.

Wagner, W. J. "May 3, 1791, and the Polish Constitutional Tradition." *Polish Review* 36, no. 4 (1991): 383–395

Walczak, Agnieszka, and Wouter van der Brug. "The Quality of Representation in European Elections." In *Proceedings of the Sixth ECPR General Conference*, University of Iceland, 2011.

Weiss, Martin A. "The Paris Club and International Debt Relief." Congressional Research Service. Washington, DC: Library of Congress, 2013.

Whalley, Alexander. "Elected Versus Appointed Policy Makers: Evidence from City Treasurers." *Journal of Law and Economics* 56, no. 1 (2013): 39–81.

Wicksell, Knut. *Finanztheoretische Untersuchungen: Nebst Darstellung und Kritik des Steuerwesens Schwedens.* G. Fischer, 1896.

Wittman, Donald A. *The Myth of Democratic Failure: Why Political Institutions Are Efficient.* Chicago: University of Chicago Press, 1995.

———. "Why Democracies Produce Efficient Results." *Journal of Political Economy* 97, no. 6 (1989): 1395–1424.

Yglesias, Matthew. "The Eurozone Is a Political Project, Not an Economic One." *Vox*, July 6, 2015.

Index